EYES TO SEE AND EARS TO HEAR WOMEN

Sexual Assault as a Crisis of Evangelical Theology

General Editor
Tim Krueger

Associate Editor
Jeff Miller

Contributing Editor
Mitch Randall

CBE International

www.cbeinternational.org

Eyes to See and Ears to Hear Women: Sexual Assault as a Crisis of Evangelical Theology

Copyright CBE International © 2018

Published by CBE International
122 W Franklin Ave, Suite 218
Minneapolis, MN 55404
www.cbeinternational.org

ISBN: 978-1-939971-80-7 (Print)
ISBN: 978-1-939971-81-4 (PDF)
ISBN: 978-1-939971-83-8 (Mobi)
ISBN: 978-1-939971-82-1 (ePub)

Cover design: Tim Krueger. Image credit: kaipong on iStock by Getty

Printed in the United States of America

CBE grants permission for any original article (not a reprint) to be photocopied for local use provided no more than 1,000 copies are made, they are distributed free, the author is acknowledged, and CBE is recognized as the source.

Please note that neither CBE International, nor the editor, nor the editorial team is responsible or legally liable for any content or any statements made by any author, but the legal responsibility is solely that author's once an article appears in print in *Eyes to See and Ears to Hear Women*.

Special thanks to Mitch Randall and the team at EthicsDaily.com for their partnership on this project.

Contents

Introduction: Eyes to See and Ears to Hear Women 1
Tim Krueger

Women Saw #MeToo Coming 100 Years Ago.
When Will We Listen? 5
Kristin Kobes Du Mez

Theological Malpractice Stands Culpable
in Sexual Abuse 13
Mitch Randall

Complementarianism:
A Separate-But-Equal Knockoff 17
Mitch Carnell

The Myth of Biblical Womanhood:
A Perspective from Medieval Africa 21
Beth Allison Barr

"Acknowledge Those Who Work Hard among You":
The Absence of Women's Work in Complementarian
Seminary Curricula 27
Chesna Hinkley

Complementarian Theology in Crisis 59
Kevin Giles

The Nashville Statement: A Critical Review 83
Jamin Hübner

About CBE International 114

TIM KRUEGER

Introduction: Eyes to See and Ears to Hear Women

On September 27, 2018, Dr. Christine Blasey Ford testified to the US Senate Judiciary Committee regarding alleged sexual assault by Supreme Court nominee Brett Kavanaugh. That day, the Rape, Abuse, and Incest National Network's sexual assault hotline got triple its normal calls.[1] Clearly, her testimony struck a chord with women across the US, many of whom have endured similar experiences. Yet, while women are keenly aware of the frequency and severity of assault, men often are unaware and skeptical.

Washington Post columnist Monica Hesse sheds light on just how ignorant fathers are about the harassment and abuse faced by their own daughters (and sons). The stories are heartbreaking:

> To the father of the junior high student who was pinned down and undressed at a gathering 30 years ago: She didn't tell you because she didn't want to see you cry. But she told me that she still remembers every detail.

To the father of the teenager who was raped at a party. You don't know about this, because she was certain that if you knew, you would kill her attacker and go to prison, and it would be her fault.

To the father of the son who was assaulted by an older man: I wish I could tell you more about what happened to him, but he wouldn't tell me, and he definitely won't tell you, because manliness is important to you, he says.[2]

Too many fathers assume that sexual assault is a rare and distant problem, not because it is but because those around them know they're unable or unwilling to handle the truth. These men's words, actions, and values signal to their loved ones that it is not safe to confide in them about sexual assault. This is bad for all involved. Children and wives bear the burden and pain of sexism and violence without the support of the men they love. Relationships suffer from a lack of honesty. Men go on reinforcing the same cultural and systemic problems that foster abuse in the first place.

But in this day, when society is being confronted with the rampant abuse all around us, men can no longer claim ignorance. The same can be said of church leaders and theologians, who, in many ways (not least because they are primarily men) are not unlike the fathers Hesse describes.

For too long, Christian leaders and Christians as a whole (particularly white men like myself) have been like Israel in the time of Jeremiah—having eyes but unable to see, having ears but unable to hear. A 2014 survey found that only 25% of pastors believed domestic violence was a problem in their congregations.[3] Given that one-third of women (and one-quarter of men) experience intimate partner violence in their lifetimes, these numbers betray a startling lack of awareness. The good news? The #MeToo movement has brought increased awareness. A 2018 Lifeway survey found that "two-thirds of pastors now say that domestic or sexual violence occurs in the lives of people in their congregation."[4]

We can no longer claim ignorance, but how will we respond? Survivor, advocate, and lawyer Rachael Denhollander observes that we have been quick to condemn abuse outside the church walls, but slow to do so within our faith communities:

My religious community applauded me for standing against Nassar and his enablers while, in the same breath, condemned me for speaking against religious institutions that mishandled abuse. . . . More often than not, we are only willing to support survivors so long as their allegations don't impinge on our community, its members, or our overall goals. But as soon as it's someone from our own tribe — when it actually costs us to care — the verbal and mental contortions ensue to explain why this allegation of abuse is "different."[5]

Will we let this pattern continue in our communities? Will we deny any role in perpetuating a culture of abuse? Or will we see, hear, and believe the prophetic and courageous women who have spoken out in this era and in the decades and centuries past? Will we stand up to abuse even when it costs us to do so? Will we repent of the ways we've been complicit and complacent? The time for change is now.

In the pages that follow, Christian scholars examine evangelicalism's engagement with women, gender, sexuality, and abuse. They find that the "complementarian" view so often touted as the biblical ideal for women and men is neither biblical nor ideal. On the contrary, it enshrines a power imbalance between men and women as God's will, centers men's voices at the expense of women's, and encourages forms of masculinity that are rooted more in patriarchal culture than the Bible. In short, while abuse occurs across the theological spectrum, this set of teachings uniquely contributes to the epidemic of sexism and abuse that have plagued the church for centuries.

We can do better. Let's imitate Jesus, who empowered women and men to lead and serve as equals. Let's become a community where a woman's word is valued as much as a man's, where forgiveness is coupled with accountability and justice. Where we not only say that women and men are equal in Christ, but finally and fully behave accordingly.

Notes

1. Donovan Slack, "Calls to sexual assault hotline jump after Christine Blasey Ford's testimony," *USA Today*, September 29, 2018, https://www.usatoday.com/story/news/politics/onpolitics/2018/09/29/christine-blasey-ford-hearing-sexual-

assault-hotline-calls-skyrocket/1471409002/.

2. Monica Hesse, "Dear dads: Your daughters told me about their assaults. This is why they never told you." *Washington Post*, October 2, 2018, https://www.washingtonpost.com/lifestyle/style/dear-dads-your-daughters-told-me-about-their-assaults-this-is-why-they-never-told-you/2018/10/01/0f69be46-c587-11e8-b2b5-79270f9cce17_story.html?noredirect=on&utm_term=.aeefe7537b7b.

3. "Broken Silence: A Call for Churches to Speak Out," Sojourners and IMA World Health, 2014, https://sojo.net/sites/default/files/Broken%20Silence%20Report.pdf.

4. Bob Smietana, "Pastors More Likely to Address Domestic Violence, Still Lack Training," Lifeway Research, September 18, 2018, https://lifewayresearch.com/2018/09/18/pastors-more-likely-to-address-domestic-violence-still-lack-training/.

5. Rachael Denhollander, "I'm a sexual assault survivor. And a conservative. The Kavanaugh hearings were excruciating," *Vox*, October 16, 2018, https://www.vox.com/first-person/2018/10/15/17968534/kavanaugh-vote-supreme-court-sexual-assault-christine-blasey-ford.

Tim Krueger is CBE's communications manager and the editor of CBE's magazine, *Mutuality*. He lives in Saint Paul, MN with his wife and two sons.

KRISTIN KOBES DU MEZ

Women Saw #MeToo Coming 100 Years Ago. When Will We Listen?

In 2018, the #MeToo movement came to American Protestantism. Emboldened with the hope that they will no longer be silenced, women are speaking out to expose the misogyny and abuse they've long endured in Christian homes, churches, and seminaries.

In recent weeks, controversy swirled around Paige Patterson and the Southern Baptist Convention. As the *Washington Post* reported,[1] the revered patriarch and now former president of Southwestern Baptist Theological Seminary fell from grace in light of revelations that he'd counseled an abused woman to stay with her husband, provocatively drawn attention to a teenage girl's appearance, and allegedly instructed a female student not to report her rape, but instead to forgive her assailant.

Upon his removal, Patterson initially received the honorary title of president emeritus and a generous compensation package. Only after widespread public outcry was this offer rescinded.

Two months before the Patterson case made the news, allegations surfaced against Bill Hybels, founding pastor of Willow Creek Community Church.[2] At least seven women accused Hybels of sexual misconduct and abuse of power. Allegations went back decades, but the church had failed to address concerns raised by multiple women over the years.

Hybels eventually resigned, and the elders expressed regret that their "process appeared to diminish the deep compassion we have for all those involved in these matters."

Just weeks before the Hybels story broke, evangelical pastor Andy Savage was in the headlines. Inspired by the #MeToo movement, Jules Woodson revealed that Savage had sexually assaulted her years earlier. She was seventeen at the time, and he was her youth pastor. When Savage confessed to a "sexual incident" in front of his Memphis congregation, he received a standing ovation.[3]

All of these stories involve the misconduct of Christian men. They reveal how men in positions of authority have abused their power, especially over women. But they also expose the Christian community's all too frequent inability or unwillingness to name abuse, to hold perpetrators accountable, and to protect and empower survivors.

The magnitude of the problem suggests that this isn't simply the case of a few wayward men. No, this problem is deeply entrenched in the core values and institutional structures of the church.

In an interview with *Christianity Today*, Rachael Denhollander offered a devastating critique of the church's failures on this front. "Church is one of the least safe places to acknowledge abuse," she insisted; because of "an abhorrent lack of knowledge for the damage and devastation that sexual assault brings," the church frequently ends up revictimizing survivors.[4]

Denhollander, who has been widely praised for her courage as the first to publicly accuse Larry Nassar of sexual abuse, encountered a very different response when she tried to address abuse within the church. When she raised concerns about the restoration of C. J. Mahaney, the former president of Sovereign Grace

Ministries accused of covering up decades of child sexual abuse within his network of churches, she and her husband were told that their church wasn't the right place for them. Had her own abuser been someone within the evangelical church, she concluded that she would have been "actively vilified and lied about by every single evangelical leader out there."

In addition to confronting decades of abuse, denial, and disregard for victims in their own churches, American evangelicals in particular must also come to terms with their public witness in light of the broader political context. In the fall of 2016, just before the presidential election and just after the release of the Access Hollywood tapes, a PRRI poll revealed that an astounding 72% of white evangelicals had decided that "a person who commits an 'immoral' act could behave ethically in a public roles."[5] PRRI's Robert P. Jones dubbed this "dramatic abandonment of the whole idea of 'value voters'…one of the most stunning reversals in recent American political history."[6] White evangelical support for Alabama Senate candidate Roy Moore, and in the wake of the Stormy Daniels revelations, continues to bear out this statistic.

All this has left American evangelicals reeling. In the words of Albert Mohler, president of Southern Baptist Theological Seminary, "The terrible swift sword of public humiliation has come with a vengeance." To Mohler, it seemed the church has suddenly come under siege: "It is as if bombs are dropping and God alone knows how many will fall and where they will land."[7]

Mohler admitted he was unprepared for "the avalanche of sexual misconduct" coming to light. Although others had warned that Catholics weren't the only ones with a problem and that evangelicals "had a similar crisis coming," he'd been dubious. "I did not see this coming," he confessed. (Perhaps he should have; two years ago, when Mahaney came under fire for covering up abuse in SGM, Mohler seemed to make light of the allegations, and chose that time to offer a ringing public endorsement of his friend.[8])

Now that the floodgates have opened, many evangelicals are finding it impossible to ignore this moment of reckoning. And many are ready to ask difficult questions:

Why do Christians—those who claim to love "family values," who claim a superior morality, who boast of honoring and "protecting" women—seem no better (and perhaps worse) than non-Christians when it comes to perpetrating acts of violence against women?

Why have "respectable," God-fearing Christians so often condoned, excused, or turned a blind eye to the abuse of women in their own churches, institutions, and communities?

Why is the church one of the least safe places for victims of sexual violence?

And, ultimately: Is the problem theological? As Mohler himself asks, is complementarianism "just camouflage for abusive males and permission for the abuse and mistreatment of women?"

Evangelicals may be surprised to learn that this isn't the first time American Christians have confronted precisely these questions.

A century ago, a woman by the name of Katharine Bushnell took up these issues in a remarkable book, *God's Word to Women*. Although few people today remember Bushnell, she was once an internationally-known evangelical anti-trafficking activist. Motivated by her deep Christian faith, Bushnell led a highly publicized campaign in the 1880s to expose the abuse of women in Wisconsin lumber camps, and a few years later she conducted a similar investigation in colonial India into the abuse of local women entrapped in British Army brothels.

In the course of this work, Bushnell was startled to discover that it was often Christian men who were guilty of perpetrating horrific violence against women. Equally troubling, she discovered that "respectable" Christian men and women all too frequently condoned that violence, blaming the victim or simply looking the other way.

Like Mohler, Bushnell was ultimately compelled to ask: Is Christian theology to blame?

Searching the Scriptures, she was drawn to passages supporting traditional notions of male headship. As I trace in my book *A New Gospel for Women: Katharine Bushnell and the Challenge of Christian Feminism* (Oxford, 2015), what puzzled Bushnell was that men who purported to follow Christ—the incarnate God who emptied himself and submitted to death on a cross—did so by claiming power over women. As she understood the gospel message, only a sinner would wish "to exalt himself and have dominion over others"—and he would do so "in exact proportion to the degree of selfishness in his heart."

Why would the Bible instruct a husband to assert authority over a wife, usurping Christ's own authority over his servants? Those who interpreted Paul's words in this way, she concluded, disregarded the "revolutionary ethics of a Christ-like love." Not one to mince words, Bushnell accused men of essentially giving free rein to their own egotism under the cover of "headship."

Bushnell did not need to reject the authority of the Scriptures in order to critique Christian patriarchy. She simply compared English translations to Hebrew and Greek texts, and discovered disturbing patterns of mistranslation when it came to key passages about women. From "the curse" of Genesis 3:16 to New Testament passages in 1 Corinthians, Ephesians, and 1 Timothy, she painstakingly demonstrated how traditional patriarchal interpretations relied on faulty translations or willful misinterpretations.

Through the ages, she discovered, Christian men had created and defended a flawed system of theology that made "one half the human family some resplendent glory which the other half is appointed to reflect and manifest forth." Conveniently, men had then assigned themselves the task of teaching this theology to the other half.

It was, after all, men who dictated that "biblical marriage" robbed women of equality and subordinated their will and wishes to their husbands. And Bushnell posited a direct connection between subordination and abuse: men would feel abused if they were enslaved to a fellow man, she reasoned, and the same was true for women, even if theologians liked to portray women's subjugation as "the happiest state in which a woman can exist."

Bushnell rejected the idea that equality and submission could go hand in hand: "The wife cannot obey while recognizing her equality with her husband, without also realizing his injustice." Bushnell also asserted that male headship was not simply a domestic matter: "Men cannot make unquestioning obedient slaves of wives only"—sooner or later this abuse of power would spill over into their dealings with all women. It was only by repudiating such false theology that women would be free to participate in "the glorious liberty of the children of God."

Bushnell's theology was in many ways revolutionary, yet some might be surprised to learn that she grounded her work in a conservative hermeneutic. She insisted that every word of the Bible was "inspired, infallible, and inviolable." And, when the fundamentalist/modernist controversy swept through American Protestantism, she sided with fundamentalists. Her book received favorable reviews from a number of conservative theologians, including a hearty endorsement published in the Moody Monthly.

The fact that a man in Mohler's position now finds himself asking if complementarian theology might be to blame for the "grievous sins" coming to light within evangelicalism is significant; conservative Southern Baptists, after all, have enshrined male headship as part of the denomination's confession of faith.

Yet perhaps too quickly, Mohler answers his own question, insisting that "the same Bible" that expresses God's "concern for the abused," also "reveals the complementarian pattern of male leadership in the home and the church." Bushnell, however, stands in a long line of Christian women who have argued that we don't need to choose between biblical fidelity and a rejection of patriarchy. And in fact, the former demands the latter.

At this moment of crisis, the church must turn its focus away from its "public humiliation." Instead, it must confront the harm done to victims of abuse and then consider how its distortion of the gospel has long enabled violence against women and a broad abuse of power in the church. To do so, we must privilege the voices of women, and recall the theology of women in history who all but predicted this reckoning.

Denhollander reminds us, "the gospel of Jesus Christ does not need your protection." Jesus requires obedience, and "obedience means that you pursue justice and you stand up for the oppressed and you stand up for the victimized, and you tell the truth about the evil of sexual assault and the evil of covering it up." This will come at a cost, but following Christ always does.

Notes

1. Bobby Ross Jr., Sarah Pulliam Bailey, and Michelle Boorstein, "Prominent Southern Baptist leader removed as seminary president following controversial remarks about abused women," *Washington Post*, May 23, 2018, https://www.washingtonpost.com/news/acts-of-faith/wp/2018/05/23/prominent-southern-baptist-leader-removed-as-seminary-president-following-controversial-remarks-about-abused-women/?noredirect=on&utm_term=.131c2ed7eee0.

2. Bob Smietana, "Willow Creek Promises Investigation Amid New Allegations Against Bill Hybels," *Christianity Today*, April 21, 2018, https://www.christianitytoday.com/news/2018/april/bill-hybels-willow-creek-promises-investigation-allegations.html.

3. Jules Woodson, "I Was Assaulted. He Was Applauded." *New York Times*, Mar. 9, 2018, https://www.nytimes.com/2018/03/09/opinion/jules-woodson-andy-savage-assault.html.

4. Interview by Morgan Lee, "My Larry Nassar Testimony Went Viral. But There's More to the Gospel Than Forgiveness," *Christianity Today*, Jan. 31, 2018, https://www.christianitytoday.com/ct/2018/january-web-only/rachael-denhollander-larry-nassar-forgiveness-gospel.html.

5. "Backing Trump, White Evangelicals Flip Flop on Importance of Candidate Character | PRRI/Brookings Survey," PRRI, Oct. 19, 2016, https://www.prri.org/research/prri-brookings-oct-19-poll-politics-election-clinton-double-digit-lead-trump/.

6. Tom Gjelten, "White Evangelicals Conflicted By Accusations Against Roy Moore," NPR, Nov. 14, 2017, https://www.npr.org/2017/11/14/563729047/white-evangelicals-conflicted-in-wake-of-roy-moore-accusations.

7. Al Mohler, "Al Mohler: The Humiliation of the Southern Baptist Convention," Christianity Today, May 23, 2018, https://www.christianitytoday.com/ct/2018/may-web-only/al-mohler-humiliation-of-southern-baptist-convention-metoo.html.

8. Al Mohler's introduction to CJ Mahaney at the Together for the Gospel Conference 2016. Online at https://soundcloud.com/watchkeep/albert-mohler-and-cj-mahaney.

This article originally appeared on CBE International's blog at https://www.cbeinternational.org/blogs/women-saw-metoo-coming-100-years-ago-when-will-we-listen, June 26, 2018.

Kristin Kobes Du Mez is a professor of history at Calvin College, and is currently writing a book on evangelical masculinity and militarism.

MITCH RANDALL

Theological Malpractice Stands Culpable in Sexual Abuse

I was one of the many Christians believing God created women for a subservient role to men.

Growing up in fundamentalist Baptist churches, it was instilled in me for more than two decades that God created women to "help" men; women were to serve their husbands and children.

This was the divine construct of God's orderly creation, supposedly a successful formula for a righteous life and happy home.

Little did I know how wrong the church was on this point, leading to what we now know as a theological culpability for sexual abuse.

Men that believe they possess a divine right to "rule" over their wives are susceptible to the "David Complex," which stems from the Old Testament narrative when King David was so overcome by his sexual desire that he forced Bathsheba to bed (2 Samuel 11).

Let's be clear: This was an abuse of power.

Bathsheba could not resist the king. If she did, Bathsheba might have faced a possible execution for treason.

In addition, David attempted to cover up his sin by having Bathsheba's husband killed in battle. The king would have gotten away with this treachery if it were not for the boldness of a prophet condemning his actions (2 Samuel 12).

The "David Complex" is not exclusive to the Old Testament. In the New Testament story of John 8, readers find Jesus condemning a male-dominionist system that believed and treated women as objects to be used and discarded.

A woman was set up to be abused by the religious male leaders of the day, just for the sake of disqualifying Jesus as a prophet.

The religious leaders only brought the woman—not the man—"caught" in adultery to him. After analyzing the situation, Jesus uttered these haunting words, "Let anyone among you who is without sin be the first to throw a stone at her."

The precision of Jesus' words is crystal-clear in the context of the story. Jesus is condemning a theology that perpetuates a patriarchal rule that leads to sexual abuse.

In other words, the sin of the religious leaders was as great as—if not worse than—the one they were condemning.

These biblical stories bring us to this extraordinary moment in time.

Over the last few months, we have witnessed one story after another where powerful men exert their authority and influence to engage in sexually abusive behaviors toward women.

While these situations are not exclusive to Christians, an argument can be made that the church has a theological culpability in these matters.

When the church teaches young girls to be subservient, the church fosters the idea that women are less important than men.

When the church argues for complementarianism (men and women have specific roles that "complement" each other), this empowers men to believe they have a distorted right to treat women in a lesser role.

When the church denies women the same rights as men when it comes to marriage, parenting, home and the church, then the church is giving society permission to treat women as a sub-class of humanity.

These church teachings are wrong and must be called out. They have contributed in creating the environment in which sexual abuse prevails under the cover of a culturally perverse mindset empowered by theological malpractice.

However, calling these ideas and behaviors immoral and wrong is not enough. As followers of Jesus, we must follow his lead in attempting a course correction when we are theologically adrift.

The church must speak out as the Old Testament prophet did when he boldly condemned King David. The church must take seriously the teachings of Jesus by pointing out systems, both secular and religious, that propagate attitudes and perspectives in which women are viewed and treated as servile objects.

The church needs to fervently promote an egalitarian theology that empowers women to fulfill their divine callings.

Equality will never be achieved as long as the church continues to turn the other way.

We must strive to do better for the young women growing up in our churches, for God's mercy may be withheld if they grow up in a church that remains silent while predators are lurking in the shadows—or in plain sight.

This article originally appeared on EthicsDaily.com's website, at https://www.ethicsdaily.com/theological-malpractice-stands-culpable-in-sexual-abuse-cms-24493/ on November 22, 2017. Used by permission.

Mitch Randall is the executive editor of EthicsDaily.com. You can follow him on Twitter @rmitchrandall.

MITCH CARNELL

Complementarianism: A Separate-But-Equal Knockoff

An article I read recently extolling the virtues of complementarianism nagged at me. It would not let me rest.

Complementarianism is a religious construct that deals with the roles of gender. The message is evil at its center.

"The SBC has affirmed complementarianism—the belief that the Bible reveals that men and women are equally made in God's image, but that men and women were also created to be complements to each other, men and women bearing distinct and different roles," Al Mohler, president of Southern Baptist Theological Seminary, stated in a recent column.[1] "This means obeying the Bible's very clear teachings on male leadership in the home and in the church."

To me, it is nothing more than the old argument of "separate but equal" applied to gender roles and dressed in a type of theological clothing. This is the same argument earlier generations used to justify segregation of the races.

The whole idea is to downgrade the role of women and to promote the superiority of men. Proponents dress it up and clothe it in statements of love. In most cases, this is window dressing.

For many, it is the excuse they need to keep women in their place.

We have been through this before: "Blacks are fine as long as they stay in their place." It stank then and it stinks now. Separate but equal was never equal, and no one pretended that it was.

The black schools in the town of my youth got hand-me-down textbooks, hand-me-down desks and chairs and rundown buildings.

We took our money to church for missionaries to win the lost in Africa, but the black children two blocks away could not come to church with us.

Under complementarianism, in many churches women can't teach men because that is not their God-prescribed role.

The inconsistency of the position is seen in the fact that female teachers teach male students in public and private schools, including religious ones, every day.

The goal is to keep women in lower paying jobs and deny them authority. The males who promote this travesty are in control and have no intention of relinquishing any of their control.

"The same Bible that reveals the complementarian pattern of male leadership in the home and the church also reveals God's steadfast and unyielding concern for the abused, the threatened, the suffering and the fearful," Mohler stated. "There is no excuse whatsoever for abuse of any form, verbal, emotional, physical, spiritual or sexual."

And yet, the nation is finally seeing some of the harmful results of this philosophy, which plays into the hands of those who abuse women around the world: "The church says that you are to obey me."

Jesus set the example for another and better way. He made it very clear that there is no artificial ranking of male and female roles in his kingdom. "Mary, go and tell my disciples."

Paul emphasized this in Galatians 3:28. "There is neither Jew nor Gentile, neither slave nor free, nor is there male and female, for you are all one in Christ Jesus."

Growing up Southern Baptist, my experience with women pastors is limited, but I have been blessed by hearing some of the best: Linda McKinnish Bridges, Amy Butler, Molly Marshall, Joan Brown Campbell, Cynthia Campbell, Julie Pennington-Russell, Susan Sparks and Martha Brown Taylor, to name only a few.

Not only have I been blessed by hearing these women, I have gained so much insight from them.

I regularly listen to and read Sparks, pastor of Madison Avenue Baptist Church in New York City.

She places God in the center of our every action and has a sense of humor and such an awareness of God's presence in the ordinary that you are compelled to listen and take notice.

McKinnish Bridges, president of Baptist Theological Seminary at Richmond, Virginia, preached her sermon, "Grace upon Grace," 27 years ago. Yet it is as fresh today as it was the first day I heard it because it expresses God's work in my life.

Marshall, president of Central Baptist Theological Seminary in Kansas, awakened my interest in the influence of the Holy Spirit in our daily lives.

Cynthia Campbell, president emerita of McCormick Theological Seminary in Chicago, preached the most inspirational sermon on the resurrection I have ever heard.

God's love for all of humanity oozes from every word from the sermons of Joan Brown Campbell, an ordained Disciples of Christ and American Baptist Church minister who was the first woman to lead the National Council of Churches.

How can you say that God rejects the work of these ambassadors of hope because they dare preach to men?

I have experienced outstanding female Bible teachers in my years in the church. You want me to disregard the teachings of these gifted women because I am a male and should not have been listening to them?

Should I have not have listened to my mother when she spoke of God's love for me? Should I have not listened to my wife when she assured me that God would watch over me and our children?

All of these women were gifted by God with talents far greater than the ones given to me. I think God brought me into contact with them because they had been given a message I was intended to hear.

I ask myself, "Where would I be in my spiritual journey if these women were not a part of my life?"

Complementarianism belongs on the ash heap of history along with separate but equal.

Notes

1. Al Mohler, "The Wrath of God Poured Out—The Humiliation of the Southern Baptist Convention" AlbertMohler.com, May 23, 2018, https://albertmohler.com/2018/05/23/wrath-god-poured-humiliation-southern-baptist-convention/.

This article originally appeared on EthicsDaily.com's website, at https://www.ethicsdaily.com/complementarianism-a-separate-but-equal-knockoff-cms-24925/ on June 11, 2018. Used by permission.

Mitch Carnell is a member of First Baptist Church of Charleston, South Carolina. He is the author of "Our Father: Discovering Family." His writings can also be found at MitchCarnell.com.

BETH ALLISON BARR

The Myth of Biblical Womanhood:

A Perspective from Medieval Africa

In 2012, Rachel Held Evans, a *New York Times* bestselling author of American Christianity, wrote a stunningly provocative book titled *A Year of Biblical Womanhood*. In it, she vividly shows us how "biblical womanhood" is not a constant. It is a culturally constructed concept.

For those of you unfamiliar with her book, she spent a year living out as many different versions of "biblical womanhood" as she could find throughout the Old and New Testaments—from sleeping in a tent in her front yard during her period to covering her head and remaining silent at church.

I would like to thank Anna Redhair Wells, who introduced me to *The Book of the Saints*. I had the privilege of directing her thesis: Anna Redhair, "Women on the move: representations of female pilgrims in medieval England and Ethiopia," master's thesis, (Baylor University, 2018).

Her book really helped me understand how biblical womanhood, to at least some degree, is in the eye of the beholder.

Today, the ideas we associate with biblical womanhood—women as submissive wives who prioritize children and home over career and who are content to teach children at church but remain under the leadership of male teachers, pastors, and husbands—are emphasized by American evangelical leaders. In truth, this idea of "biblical womanhood" owes as much (if not more) to Western cultural norms of the last 200 years than it does to the Bible.

Yet, this truth has not sunk in among many evangelical Christians. Indeed, it often seems that the opposite has happened—rather than a cultural construction, "biblical womanhood" is viewed as integral to normative Christianity.

In a 2012 interview, for example, John Piper, Denny Burke, and Tim Keller argued that male headship and female submission is not a secondary issue; it is a gospel issue. Keller argued that complementarianism, the view that God designed distinct roles for men and women in both biology and personhood, "indirectly affects the way we understand scripture and the way we understand the gospel." Piper cut to the chase, stating the "men are wired to lead," and if Christians "aren't willing to stand against the tide" of culture on this issue (i.e. support complementarianism and reject egalitarianism), "you are probably going to cave on some other important issues."[1]

In other words, what you believe about male headship and female submission is a litmus test for orthodoxy.

Those who support more egalitarian readings of Scripture, Piper suggests, are more likely to compromise the gospel. Those who accept "biblical womanhood," in contrast, are more likely to be theologically sound.

Men lead; women follow. The Bible (not just a particular interpretation of some biblical texts; but the Bible) tells us so. Not long ago, Desiring God posted this remark by John Piper on Facebook:

> Leadership is taking initiative. Who says, "Let's . . ." more often in your relationship? "Let's go out to eat." "Let's try to get our finances in order." "Let's get to church on time next Sunday." Who says it most often? If it's the wife, you have a problem, and the problem is with the guy. If it's the guy, she's probably happy, because she doesn't want to be the one to say "let's"

over and over again. In general, leadership means a bent toward initiative under which women thrive.²

This post got over 1,700 responses, mostly "likes" and "loves." It was shared 430 times (at my last count). While I can't prove that most of these likes and loves were evangelical Christians, I am probably right that they are.

Conservative evangelical Christians support male headship and associate "biblical womanhood" with marriage, family, and submission.

As I have argued previously, only a handful of verses are used to define this notion of biblical womanhood: 1 Corinthians 11 and 14, Ephesians 5, 1 Timothy 2, and Colossians 3.³ These verses have become increasingly popular since the 1950s. They also have been increasingly used as the primary lens through which conservative Christians view women.

Yet, as I have also argued, the emphasis on Paul's writings about women—specifically 1 Corinthians 11 and 14, Colossians 3, Ephesians 5, and 1 Timothy 2—has been far less consistent throughout church history than many evangelicals like to think.⁴

Evidence from vernacular sermons in late medieval England shows that Paul's writings about women have not always been in the forefront of Christian thought. Nor have they always been applied to limit female authority.

This lack of concern for either emphasizing female subordination or arguing against female leadership becomes even more apparent when we turn to *The Book of the Saints of the Ethiopian Church*.⁵ This collection of more than 1,000 saints' lives, compiled probably in the thirteenth century, and created to be read regularly during church services, has remained a significant part of Ethiopian Christianity since the medieval era.

In the book, Scripture is regularly woven into the stories of the saints, including at least thirty-two specific references to Paul and his writings. From stories about Paul in Acts to Scripture incorporated from Corinthians, Galatians, Timothy, Romans, etc., the writings of Paul form both a familiar and a critical part of this religious text.

Yet like the sermons in late medieval England, *The Book of the Saints* is absolutely silent on the Pauline scripture referencing female subordination and limiting female authority. It is simply not there.

What is there, however, is clear support for women exercising leadership roles. Let me share just two examples from *The Book of the Saints*: the stories of Thecla and Sara of Antioch.

Thecla

Thecla lived in Macedonia during the first century and heard Paul preach what seems to be a part of the Sermon on the Mount: "Blessed are those who are poor for righteousness' sake, for theirs is the kingdom of heaven. Blessed are those who mourn here for they shall rejoice. Blessed are those who are persecuted for righteousness' sake, for theirs is the kingdom of heaven." When Thecla heard these words, she converted to Christianity and sneaked out to meet Paul. Paul welcomed her, absolutely unconcerned about her female body or her female personhood (she definitely wasn't adhering to modern notions of "biblical womanhood"), and taught her.

When her parents and the government tried to arrest her for illegally converting to Christianity, she miraculously escaped and ran off to join Paul. He again took her in. Just as Jesus welcomed Mary of Bethany and taught her like a man (she sat at the feet of the teacher and ignored her household responsibilities) even though she was a woman, Paul welcomed Thecla. She followed him, learned from him, performed miracles, and—in the words of the text—"preached in the Name of the Lord Jesus Christ." This is exactly the phrase used to describe Paul's preaching—"he began to preach in the Name of the Lord Jesus Christ." Thecla "continued to follow Paul, and to preach in the Name of Our Lord Jesus Christ." Instead of teaching "women be silent" or "women should not exercise authority over men," *The Book of the Saints* affirms a woman as a disciple of the apostle Paul, a preacher in exactly the same way as the Paul, and a leader of the early church in her own right.

If God created women distinct in biology and personhood (designed to perform different roles from men, especially in regards to family and leadership), why could Thecla defy her family and be trained by Paul to become a leader in the early church—disciple, missionary, preacher? Moreover her story was used as an exemplar for both women and men in medieval Ethiopia. The text makes no indication that she was to be considered anomalous. In fact, it doesn't really matter to the text that she was a woman. Rather it was her conversion, devotion, and leadership. *Biblical womanhood?*

Sara of Antioch

My second story likewise advances a different picture of biblical womanhood. This time, the woman is a mother, but she defies the authority of her husband, becomes the faith leader in her own family, and overturns the authority of a priest. The story is of a holy saint named Sara from Antioch. Her husband was a governor of Diocletian. His family converted to Christianity, but when the emperor confronted him, the man became an apostate. He told his Sara, "I love the Faith of Christ, but I denied Him, because I am afraid of the emperor's torturings."

Sara, however, did not follow in her husband's footsteps. She became concerned about the salvation of her sons, given the example of their father. So she ran away with them to Alexandria to find the archbishop and ask him to baptize her sons. On the way, a terrible storm struck and their ship began to sink. Sara prayed for God to help her. Then she took a razor, slit her breast, and used her own blood to anoint her sons with the sign of the cross. She then dipped them three times over the side of the ship into the sea, proclaiming their baptism in the "Name of the Father and the Son and the Holy Spirit." The sea immediately grew calm.

After arriving at Alexandria, Sara took her children to the archbishop. He was administering a large baptism, and so she pulled her boys into the line. Funny enough, however, when he tried to scoop water out of the font to baptize them, the water congealed. He was confused. So he tried again. The same thing happened. Finally, he brought Sara in for questioning. She confessed that she, a woman, had already baptized her sons (not to mentioning performing a miracle by calming the sea). She begged for forgiveness, presumably for taking over the role of a priest. The archbishop, however, refused her confession. She had done nothing wrong. As he said, "Fear not, for it is our Lord Jesus Christ Who hath baptized thy sons, with His own hand, when thou didst immerse them in the sea." Interestingly, the language he used is very similar to an ancient text called the *Didascalia* (which authorizes the role of deaconess). It stated that deacons stood in for Jesus Christ. In the same way, this woman stood in for Jesus Christ and her baptism was accepted as efficacious.

These medieval religious stories from Ethiopia absolutely ignored the Pauline proscriptions and household codes. Instead of emphasizing female subordination, they emphasized women in leadership roles—as teacher, as preacher, as baptizer.

Could it be that the complementarian notion of "biblical womanhood" (especially the claim that women's distinct personhood makes no room for women as teachers and leaders of men) is a recent, Western perspective?

Could our modern notion of "biblical womanhood," which confines women's primary role to house and family and forbids women all leadership roles over men in the church, have less to do with the Bible and more to do with US Christianity?

Think about it.

Notes

1. The video is posted at Denny Burk, "How Complementarianism Is a Gospel Issue," DennyBurk.com, August 16, 2012, http://www.dennyburk.com/why-complementarianism-is-a-gospel-issue/.

2. Desiring God's Facebook page, April 27, 2018, accessed May 2, 2018, https://www.facebook.com/DesiringGod/posts/10156944636074240.

3. See Beth Allison Barr, "Paul on Women: A Modern Obsession?," *The Anxious Bench* (blog), February 21, http://www.patheos.com/blogs/anxiousbench/2018/02/paul-on-women-a-modern-obsession/ and Beth Allison Barr, "Paul Interrupted: A Medieval Perspective" *The Anxious Bench* (blog), March 21, 2018, http://www.patheos.com/blogs/anxiousbench/2018/03/paul-interrupted-a-medieval-perspective/.

4. Barr, "Paul Interrupted."

5. Ya'Ityopyā 'ortodoks tawāḥedo béta kerestiyān, and E. A. Wallis Budge, *The Book of the Saints of the Ethiopian Church: A Translation of the Ethiopic Synaxarium Maṣḥafa Senkesār [transliterated from Ethiopic]* (Cambridge: University Press, 1928).

A version of this article first appeared on The Anxious Bench, *at http://www.patheos.com/blogs/anxiousbench/2018/05/the-myth-of-biblical-womanhood-a-perspective-from-medieval-africa/. Used by permission.*

Beth Allison Barr earned her PhD in medieval history from the University of North Carolina at Chapel Hill in 2004 and currently is an associate professor of history and director of graduate studies in history at Baylor University. Her research focuses on women and gender in late medieval and early modern English sermons. You can follow her on Twitter @bethallisonbarr.

CHESNA HINKLEY

"Acknowledge Those Who Work Hard among You":
The Absence of Women's Work in Complementarian Seminary Curricula

At the height of this year's outcry over Paige Patterson's long pattern of sexism and mishandling abuse, it seemed like complementarianism might face a reckoning. For all the happy, mutually respectful couples who identify as complementarian, can a system that rests on women's essentially submissive nature really keep them safe when something goes wrong? At a deeper level, can a system that bans women from participation in certain ministries of the church produce a sustainable culture of respect for women? The answer, it seems to me, lies partially in the way the theology is *applied* to "exceptional" situations by its boots-on-the-ground practitioners—pastors.

Patterson is not the only pastor—nor the only famous pastor—to set an example of misogynistic and dangerous appropriation of complementarianism at those crucial moments when a philosophical system is shown to be *ethically viable or bankrupt*. Whether he acted in line with some sort of "pure" complementarianism or not, systems like this one, that in practice are highly relevant to the lives of the whole church, do not exist in a vacuum. Instead, they are partially *constituted* by the actions of those who define their terms. Patterson, until recently, was one of those powerful evangelicals whose ministries and writings inform what complementarianism is, and his position as an educator gave him great sway over the formation of those who would preach and practice it all over the world.

Two weeks before Patterson was forced to resign as president of Southwestern Baptist Theological Seminary, historian Beth Allison Barr responded to the situation with research on Southern Baptist (SBC) education published on her blog.[1] Positing that a failure to understand women's place in Christian history was behind the toxic brand of sexism that eventually brought Patterson down, she looked at the Southwestern Baptist Theological Seminary (SWBTS) course catalog to find out what men were learning as they prepared to be pastors.

Barr found eight courses on history and four that mentioned women among the 148 offered that semester. She also counted content on women in the history textbooks being used, and found that 98.6% of primary sources (all but one) and 94% of the content of the secondary sourcebook concerned men.[2] Barr suggests that without any knowledge of women in church history, nor much of history in general, SBC pastors are left assuming that women play little or no role in Christian history and ought to play diminished ones in today's church. In a chapter for a forthcoming edition of *Discovering Biblical Equality*, Mimi Haddad argues that disinterest in women's history plagues the Evangelical Theological Society (ETS) in a similar way, leading to incorrect and androcentric assumptions among evangelicals. I provided research for this chapter on ETS conference and journal content, which forms part of the data reported in this paper.

I am further concerned that people are led to believe that complementarianism is "traditional"—a misconception that allows the inconsistencies at the heart of the system to be treated as longstanding spiritual mysteries instead of recent logical flaws. I expanded Barr's project to fifteen conservative seminaries, including SWBTS, as well as to all the history content published by the Evangelical Theological Society in the last thirty years. At each seminary, I investigate not just history, but all departments, as well as faculty. While I agree with Barr's contention that a lack of historical awareness contributes to sexism in the church, I further find that women's issues are systematically compartmentalized, women's academic work is ignored or suppressed, women faculty are not treated as equals, and academic interest in women is primarily directed toward the maintenance of male power. Across multiple disciplines, men are educated for ministry that both overlooks women's work and blames them for problems, while asking students to uphold a system of thought that is logically flawed and inconsistent with experience. The knowledge of God, meanwhile, is misappropriated as a possession of men, rather than a gift of the Spirit.

Methods

Women in History at ETS [3]

I read through issues of the *Journal of the Evangelical Theological Society* from 1988 through the first issue in 2018, counting all the history-related articles and reviews of history-related books. I did the same with conference programs from ETS annual meetings for the years 1998–2000, 2002–05, and 2007–17. ETS informed me that conference programs no longer exist for the meetings through 1997, in 2001, and in 2006. I excluded content from the Evangelical Philosophical Society, which shares meeting space and lists its sessions in the program.

Women in All Subjects at Evangelical Seminaries

Sample

As my sample, I chose fifteen Protestant seminaries with conservative views on biblical inerrancy. Broadly, they represent four streams of Reformation thought. I selected three Reformed schools, one of which is the only official seminary of the Presbyterian Church in America (PCA). The other two frequently educate PCA pastors. Both schools affiliated with the Anglican Church in North America (ACNA) are on the list, as well as both connected with the Lutheran Church Missouri Synod (LCMS). I included all six Southern Baptist Convention (SBC) seminaries and finally, two non-denominational schools. Bethlehem College and Seminary is important to any complementarian sample, as John Piper is its chancellor, and it maintains the most exclusionary admissions policies of any school on this list by banning women from all its graduate programs. Bob Jones University is a relatively close approximation of what I expected to find at the influential Liberty University Rawlings School of Divinity, with a far more manageable dataset. Bob Jones is certainly stricter in its views on gender than is Liberty, but is known for many of the same commitments to social and political conservatism and falls within a similar sector of evangelicalism. These schools vary in their attitudes toward women in ministry, though most state complementarian views.

- Westminster Theological Seminary, founded by dissenting professors during the Princeton controversy of the early twentieth century
- Reformed Theological Seminary (RTS), which educates a large number of PCA pastors
- Covenant Theological Seminary, affiliated with the PCA
- Trinity School for Ministry, affiliated with the ACNA, which ordains women to the priesthood (not as bishops) by local option, but is led by a complementarian archbishop
- Nashotah House Theological Seminary, affiliated with the ACNA
- Concordia Seminary, St. Louis, affiliated with the complementarian LCMS
- Concordia Theological Seminary, Fort Wayne, affiliated with the LCMS
- Southern Baptist Theological Seminary (SBTS), affiliated with the SBC
- Southwestern Baptist Theological Seminary (SWBTS), affiliated with the SBC
- Southeastern Baptist Theological Seminary (SEBTS), affiliated with the SBC
- Midwestern Baptist Theological Seminary (MBTS), affiliated with the SBC
- New Orleans Baptist Theological Seminary (NOBTS), affiliated with the SBC

- Gateway Seminary of the SBC
- Bob Jones Seminary and Graduate School of Religion, an independent fundamentalist Baptist school
- Bethlehem College and Seminary, founded as an expansion of Bethlehem Baptist Church's leadership training program.

Curricula

For each school, I read through the most recent available course catalog, counting courses into five broad divisions:

- *Theology*, including systematic theology, ethics, apologetics, world religions, and philosophy
- *Biblical studies*, including Old and New Testament, archaeology, and hermeneutics
- *History*, including, because of the frequency with which it is the only history offered, historical theology
- *Practical topics*, including, but not limited to, homiletics, pastoral care, evangelism, spiritual formation, Christian education, and worship
- *Other*. A few topics, such as bioethics, creative writing, and homemaking, fall into the "other" category, and I have also placed women's studies, where distinct from women's ministry, in this section.

For each of these divisions, I counted all the courses that are either *on women* or *for women only*. I suspected from the outset that many courses that might refer to women or their issues would be about marriage and sexuality or would be limited to women, and I have separated these as far as possible from general curriculum courses *about* women. Of course, because schools usually release a new catalog every year, it is possible that all of these seminaries offer classes on women every second year that I did not count. I excluded internships, practica, independent study, and languages (except exegesis courses). Because some schools also offer degrees for licensing in non-ministry fields, I also eliminated education, music, and counseling courses, where not explicitly directed toward congregational ministry.

Faculty

Finally, I counted the faculty, including adjuncts, at each school, deferring to the catalog when its list differed from that elsewhere on the school's website. In the case of schools that offer undergraduate programs, these faculty are included, as many teach in both programs and I consider women teaching in the undergraduate program relevant to a school's attitude toward women faculty. This also allowed me to report the highest possible figure for each school. The undergraduate programs offered at these schools are typically accessory to the school's primary purpose as a seminary. The exception is Bob Jones, where the seminary constitutes a department in an otherwise established university; only religion professors are counted here, though they may teach undergraduate and/or graduate students. I counted as "non-adjunct" anyone at or above the assistant professor rank and visiting professors. I calculated gender ratios for each school and as a composite figure. I also consulted the Association of Theological Schools' (ATS) reported gender distributions. ATS reports only full-time faculty in seminary/divinity school programs, so its figure cannot perfectly correspond to my composite total percentage for all faculty in undergraduate and graduate programs at these fifteen schools. However, it is worth noting that women typically make up a greater proportion of adjuncts than of tenured faculty—women with young children, in particular, are 35% less likely to land a tenure-track position than men in the same situation[4]—and for that reason I expect the ATS figure I report here would be higher if adjuncts were included. At the same time, the figure for these fifteen schools would be lower if only seminary professors were counted. Thus, while this comparison is not flawless, more data would not improve the picture for these schools, but only push the figures further apart than they already are.

Results

Table 1. The Evangelical Theological Society's output of women's history as a percentage of all history content, 1988-2018

Evangelical Theological Society[5]	On history	On women's history	% women's history
ETS meeting (1998–2000, 2002–05, 2007–17): plenary address	9	0	0.00
ETS meeting (1998-2000, 2002-05, 2007–17): workshop/individual paper	995	21	2.11
JETS (1988: no. 1–2018: no. 1): journal article	98	2	2.04
JETS (1988: no. 1–2018: no. 1): book review	225	6	2.67
Total	1327	29	2.19

Table 2. Faculty by gender: at 15 seminaries, as a composite figure, and as reported by the Association of Theological Schools

School	Non-Adjunct	Women	Adjunct	Women	Total	Women	%
Westminster[6]	29	0	44	2	73	2	2.74
RTS[7]	87	4	20	3	107	7	6.54
Covenant (PCA)[8]	21	1	6	2	27	3	11.11
Bob Jones[9]	21	0	5	0	26	0	0.00
Bethlehem College and Seminary[10]	16	1	12	2	28	3	10.71
Trinity School for Ministry (ACNA)[11]	23	3	n/a	n/a	23	3	13.04
Nashotah House (ACNA)[12]	11	0	5	0	16	0	0.00
Concordia–St. Louis (LCMS)[13]	58	0	n/a	n/a	58	0	0.00
Concordia–Ft. Wayne (LCMS)[14]	32	0	20	1	52	1	1.92
SBTS (SBC)[15]	113	6	4	0	117	6	5.13
SWBTS (SBC)[16]	103	9	n/a	n/a	103	9	8.74
SEBTS (SBC)[17]	84	3	22	2	106	5	4.72
MBTS (SBC)[18]	24	1	n/a	n/a	24	1	4.17
NOBTS (SBC)[19]	83	10	44	14	127	24	18.90
Gateway (SBC)[20]	53	5	116	11	169	16	9.47
Total	758	43	298	37	1056	80	7.58
Total reported to the Association of Theological Schools in 2017[21]	3449	857	n/a	n/a	3449	857	24.85

Table 3. Courses and programs restricted by gender.

School[22]	Beliefs on gender	Enrollment in some courses restricted to men	Enrollment in some degree programs restricted to men
Westminster	Complementarian	Yes	Yes: Master of Divinity (Pastoral Ministry track) and Doctor of Ministry (Pastoral Ministry and Preaching tracks)
RTS	Complementarian	Yes	No
Covenant	Complementarian	Yes	No
Bob Jones	Complementarian	Yes	Yes: Professional Ministry Studies division (education for non-degreed working pastors)
Bethlehem	Complementarian	Yes	Yes: women are not admitted to any seminary degree program
Trinity	None stated	No	No
Nashotah House	None stated	No	No
Concordia–St. Louis	Complementarian	Yes	Yes: Master of Divinity, Master of Sacred Theology, and Doctor of Ministry
Concordia–Ft. Wayne	Complementarian	Yes	Yes: Master of Divinity and Doctor of Ministry
SBTS	Complementarian	Yes	Yes: Master of Divinity (Pastoral Studies track)
SWBTS	Complementarian	Yes	No
SEBTS	Complementarian	Yes	No
MBTS	Complementarian	Yes	No
NOBTS	Complementarian	Yes	No
Gateway	Complementarian	Yes	No

Table 4. Percent of courses by topical grouping at 15 seminaries and as composite figures.

School[24]	Total	Practical	% Practical	Theology	% Theology	Biblical	% Biblical	History	% History	Other	% Other
Westminster	152	43	28.3	47	30.9	38	25.0	24	15.8	0	0.0
RTS	178	59	33.1	46	25.8	55	30.9	18	10.1	0	0.0
Covenant	68	40	58.8	7	10.3	17	25.0	4	5.9	0	0.0
Bob Jones	91	28	30.8	18	19.8	38	41.8	7	7.7	0	0.0
Bethlehem	40	16	40.0	10	25.0	12	30.0	2	5.0	0	0.0
Trinity	44	13	29.5	16	36.4	10	22.7	5	11.4	0	0.0
Nashotah House	36	12	33.3	6	16.7	10	27.8	8	22.2	0	0.0
Concordia–St. Louis	77	25	32.5	16	20.8	19	24.7	17	22.1	0	0.0
Concordia–Ft. Wayne	162	38	23.5	40	24.7	40	24.7	44	27.2	0	0.0
SBTS	259	137	46.6	43	14.6	55	18.7	24[25]	8.2	0	0.0
SWBTS	509	215	42.2	80	15.7	150	29.5	35	6.9	29	5.7
SEBTS	298	161	54.0	62	20.8	33	11.1	37	12.4	5	1.7
MBTS	276	130	47.1	36	13.0	91	33.0	19	6.9	0	0.0
NOBTS	423	221	52.2	52	12.3	132	31.2	18	4.3	0	0.0
Gateway	246	135	54.9	24	9.8	63	25.6	24	9.8	0	0.0
Total	**2859**	**1273**	**44.5**	**503**	**17.6**	**763**	**26.7**	**286**	**10.0**	**34**	**1.2**

Table 5. Practical courses having to do with women or limited to women.

School[26]	Practical	On women	% Women	For women only	% Women only
Westminster	43	1	2.3	0	0.0
RTS	59	0	0.0	1	1.7
Covenant	40	0	0.0	0	0.0
Bob Jones	28	0	0.0	1	3.6
Bethlehem	16	0	0.0	0	0.0
Trinity	13	0	0.0	0	0.0
Nashotah House	12	0	0.0	0	0.0
Concordia–St. Louis	25	1	4.0	0	0.0
Concordia–Ft. Wayne	38	0	0.0	9	23.7
SBTS	137	0	0.0	0	0.0
SWBTS	215	6	2.8	3	1.4
SEBTS	161	6	3.7	6	3.7
MBTS	130	0	0.0	0	0.0
NOBTS	221	17	7.7	12	5.4
Gateway	135	4	3.0	0	0.0
Total	**1273**	**35**	**2.7**	**32**	**2.5**

Table 6. Theology courses having to do with women.

School[27]	Theology	On women	% Women
Westminster	47	0	0.0
RTS	46	0	0.0
Covenant	7	0	0.0
Bob Jones	18	0	0.0
Bethlehem	10	0	0.0
Trinity	16	0[28]	0.0
Nashotah House	6	0	0.0
Concordia–St. Louis	16	0	0.0
Concordia–Ft. Wayne	40	0	0.0
SBTS	43	0	0.0
SWBTS	80	0	0.0
SEBTS	62	1	1.6
MBTS	36	1	2.8
NOBTS	52	0	0.0
Gateway	24	0	0.0
Total	**503**	**2**	**0.4**

Table 7. Biblical studies courses having to do with women.

School[29]	Biblical Studies	On Women	% On Women
Westminster	38	0	0.0
RTS	55	2[30]	3.6
Covenant	17	0	0.0
Bob Jones	38	1[31]	2.6
Bethlehem	12	0	0.0
Trinity	10	0	0.0
Nashotah House	10	0	0.0
Concordia–St. Louis	19	0	0.0
Concordia–Ft. Wayne	40	0	0.0
SBTS	55	1	1.8
SWBTS	150	4[32]	2.7
SEBTS	33	1	3.0
MBTS	91	0	0.0
NOBTS	132	4[33]	3.0
Gateway	63	1	1.6
Total	**763**	**14**	**1.8**

Table 8. History courses having to do with women.

School[34]	History	On Women	% On Women
Westminster	24	0	0.0
RTS	18	0	0.0
Covenant	4	0	0.0
Bob Jones	7	0	0.0
Bethlehem	2	0	0.0
Trinity	5	0	0.0
Nashotah House	8	0	0.0
Concordia–St. Louis	17	0	0.0
Concordia–Ft. Wayne	44	3[35]	6.8
SBTS	24	0	0.0
SWBTS	35	0[36]	0.0
SEBTS	37	2	5.4
MBTS	19	0	0.0
NOBTS	18	2	11.1
Gateway	24	1	4.2
Total	**286**	**8**	**2.8**

Table 9. Other courses having to do with women or limited to women.

School[37]	Other	On women	% On Women	For Women Only	% For Women Only
SWBTS	29	14 (overlap of 2)	48.3	7 (overlap of 2)	24.1
SEBTS	5	0	0.0	1	20.0
Total	**34**	**14 (overlap of 2)**	**41.2**	**8 (overlap of 2)**	**23.5**

Discussion

Women in History at ETS

The Evangelical Theological Society's output of women's history is consistent across multiple datasets at just over two percent of all history content. Some of these concern married couples of whom the husband is the better known figure, and less than half are about individual female figures in history. In contrast to the mere twenty-nine articles, book reviews, and conference presentations on women in the whole history of the church, over the same period I counted 137 on Jonathan Edwards alone.

While a quick glance over any conference program for the past several years indicates ETS is quite interested in *gender*, it is not, evidently, much interested in women. There is plenty of discussion on the theological foundations for preserving male authority and preeminence, and some tolerance of opposing viewpoints on *that* question. However, this reduces women to an abstract "role" in a discussion of what is proper to them in a generally essentialist framework. The reality of women's work, faith, theology, and experiences is apparently irrelevant.[38] Women matter academically insofar as the roles they occupy matter—justification and maintenance of gender hierarchy, rather than the pursuit of knowledge, are the major concerns. This is one among many manifestations of a fault-line problem in complementarian discussion of women: disinterested commentary on real women who have done something of value is rare.

Rather, women are fawned over as a group for their "unique contributions," or men are overly concerned that women understand how valuable their (technically powerless) input is. This anxiety to make women feel better may stem from unconscious guilt over the artificial power imbalance of complementarianism when compared with men's experience of women. However, I suspect ignorance of the authority and influence women have exerted in, for example, such major events as the Council of Constantinople, the translation of the Vulgate, the clerical morality scandals of the eleventh century, and the theological and political affairs of the Reformation. Complementarianism assumes a circumscribed role for women that does not allow for the preaching, theological writing, and authority historical awareness would expose.

For men who assume they are preserving Christian tradition with complementarianism, women's history is naturally a "special interest" topic—a concession made when there is nothing more important to discuss. If it is true that women participating in public ministry is a recent capitulation to modern culture, then women's history is not likely to be of much interest to anyone other than women. On the other hand, if history about women were a more common topic of discussion, I imagine there would be a shift in complementarians' perception of women's abilities, the importance of their ministry to the whole church, and what may be said to be "traditional," theologically and otherwise.

Women in All Subjects at Evangelical Seminaries

Across all departments and all fifteen schools, courses about women constitute 2.2% of the total. These courses make up 0.4% of theology, 1.8% of biblical studies, 2.8% of history, 2.7% of practical topics, and 41.2% of "other" courses. The Women's Studies department at SWBTS explains the high percentage in the "other" category, because at SWBTS it is distinct from Women's Ministry ("practical"). However, this exposes the compartmentalization of "women's issues," as the department collects women's history, theology of womanhood, and women in the Bible while being at least partially limited to women. Even those courses that are not technically closed to men are effectively labeled "non-essential" by their relegation to a special department with which no male degree candidate is ever required to interact. In this vein, of the eight schools that do not have any special "women's degree," five have not a single class on women. Among the other three, Westminster offers one elective course on the "role" of women in the church, and Bob Jones and RTS offer one and two, respectively, which study the books of Ruth and Esther. As at ETS, women themselves are a women's interest, not essential to a man's education, nor to a pastor.

Faculty

Rarely did a school volunteer its statistics for enrollment by gender, though racial and ethnic distributions were generally available. The exception is Westminster, which reports 82% male students.[39] Publishing gender ratios among admissions information is generally an attempt by a school to appear welcoming to women. Equity, or even the appearance of it, is evidently not a priority for these seminaries. In fact, Bethlehem's published non-discrimination policy fails to mention discrimination on the basis of gender—a conspicuous omission, given that it is highly unusual.[40]

New Orleans Baptist Theological Seminary has the highest percentage of female faculty (18.9%), though it is worth noting that it also has the most women's ministry courses. Even this figure, significantly larger than that at most of the schools, falls six points lower than that reported for all schools accredited by ATS. Furthermore, more than half of NOBTS's female faculty are adjuncts, whom ATS does not count (see Methods). Taken together, these fifteen schools report 7.58% female faculty, with 20% of these seminaries employing no female professors at all. Counting only non-adjuncts, women make up just 5.67%, while ATS reports 24.85% female full-time faculty at schools it accredits—proportionally more than *four times* those at these fifteen seminaries. ATS also reports that 27.7% of those completing doctoral degrees are women.[41] Furthermore, women at these seminaries are often teaching women's ministry, women's studies, counseling, or education. Women are rare on the faculty of departments that teach theological topics to men. In fact, Reformed Theological Seminary explicitly bans women from serving on its faculties in theology, practical theology, and biblical studies.[42]

Even as it seems impossible for qualified women to gain a footing in departments these seminaries regard as central, those women who teach other women are often not required to hold the same credentials as their male colleagues who teach men. For example, 92% of RTS' male faculty is at least a candidate for a terminal degree, compared to 28.6% of the female faculty. Southern Baptist Theological Seminary's Distinguished Professor of Women's Studies has not received a doctoral degree, and even her bachelor's degree is totally unrelated to the department in which she teaches.[43] The requirement that SBC faculty, in particular, affirm complementarianism no doubt shrinks the pool of highly-educated female candidates significantly, but I doubt the problem is limited to this. Rather, women are, again, a women's concern—auxiliary to the serious work of men and not particularly important. Rigor and credibility among women, and among those who teach them, are also not particularly important. The purpose of many of these courses is to tell women how to be the kind of inoffensive wives they believe men want.

What does this do for male students at complementarian seminaries? Men who train at these schools learn nothing about women academically, leaving them with the impression that women have been unimportant—indeed, unnecessary—throughout Christian history, that they do not contribute to theology, and that their pastoral care can be left to other women, who typically are neither paid nor trained. Because they are also not compelled to learn from female faculty in their graduate program, their field becomes, in their minds, a masculine one. They are never asked to see women as theologically astute or even competent, and certainly not as authority figures. Since most of these new pastors will go on to churches where women do not enjoy the same rights and opportunities as men, many will never experience a female supervisor or even a colleague on the same level. They will never interact with women on an equal basis in a professional capacity. Women then matter as objects of male ministry or as assistants to men, but not in any capacity that does not refer to men. In fact, not a few complementarians have openly said that women were *created* for the purposes of men.[44] Besides the implications for ministry, these problems perpetuate the male curriculum bias through those men who go on to teach at seminaries.

Special Programs for Women

Southern Baptist seminaries in particular are given to providing programs, and sometimes formal academic certificates, on how to be a "ministry wife." There are classes for missionaries' wives, pastors' wives, and even seminary students' wives. SBTS offers the Seminary Wives Institute—a non-degree program in which women take modified versions of a few seminary classes alongside courses on being a woman. Similarly, there are the Seminary Studies for Student Wives program (SWBTS), the Biblical Women's Institute (SEBTS), and the Midwestern Women's Institute (MBTS). However they may advertise themselves, these programs are not offered to provide any theological education, rather, they exist to teach women how to behave. Several courses concern "biblical womanhood," a phrase that is loaded with decades of controversy but usually implies a dim view of working mothers. A large proportion are simply about being a wife, which means that this is perceived as a more delicate and easier botched project than being a husband (courses on how to be a good husband are exceedingly rare, although the question is raised in pastoral lifestyle classes at a couple of schools). This is in keeping with the general sense that to be a wife is to have a vocation, while to be a husband is to have an assistant. The woman, since the marriage is her job, for which she was educated, is far more likely to be blamed for marital problems, which is in fact what we frequently see from complementarians. Paige Patterson and his many defenders are this year's best example, but anyone who has ever told a woman to submit in order to fix her husband's bad behavior typifies this attitude.

Programs Limited to Men

Some seminaries ban women from the MDiv program entirely. LCMS seminaries do not admit women to the STM or DMin either, which may explain why it is so frequent that their female professors have no doctorate. Women at these schools are admitted to the MA for deaconess certification, in which are several courses about women that are closed to men. Bethlehem does not admit women to any of its graduate programs. Westminster and a few SBC schools have pastoral ministry tracks within the MDiv program from which women are barred. The most generous interpretation of this is that the school is making an effort to give future pastors an education totally focused on pastoring, whereas many MDiv programs also cater to academics and those going into a variety of ministries. However, in most of these contexts, advanced theological study is, practically, less important for women. Piper would prefer that no woman ever teach theological topics to men, so why would Bethlehem be interested in graduate theological education for women?[45]

On the other hand, this is also a convenient way to keep women out of certain courses without explicitly stating that they are not allowed to register for them. For example, Westminster bans women from the pastoral ministry track, and students outside this track from preaching classes. This is unfortunate for everyone involved, as it means that people who are qualified to be considered for ordination—men in the other MDiv tracks—have not taken a preaching class. A more common method of dealing with this problem is to have separate preaching or pastoral classes for men and women. The women's courses, naturally, are not called "preaching;" there are a number of creative names for them. RTS offers the apparently identical "Exegesis and Homiletics" (for men) and "Exegesis and Communication" (for women). SWBTS offers "Expository Communication of Biblical Truth" for women, with a lower course number than its introductory preaching class. I am hard-pressed to see how "expository communication of biblical truth" can be defined as anything but preaching—but surely if it does not "count," women could do it with male classmates in the room? It is almost as if they consider it immodest for women to speak about the Bible. Similarly, MBTS diverts women from "Pastoral Leadership" and "Introduction to Pastoral Ministry" to "Principles of Leadership" and "Introduction to Adult Ministry." Even when women are admitted to the program, anxiety about what they are "allowed" to do necessitates ridiculous semantic distinctions—consonant with the anachronistic assertion that the Bible limits all "ordained ministry" to men.[46] Some schools simply suggest women substitute an elective in place of preaching, in which case they are receiving a less robust education for the same degree. In any of these scenarios, men are never required to hear a woman preach, nor even to "exposit biblical truth." This is just one way in which being made to feel "special" is part of these men's professional (and spiritual) formation.

Practical vs. Academic

A large majority (84.5%) of courses for or about women are either "practical" or "other." In some sense, this is reasonable—courses about ministry to women are more pressing and varied, probably, than courses about womanhood as a theological topic, which is the only way in which women show up in other departments. On the other hand, this means there are no courses about female theologians, very few about women in history, and almost none about women in the Bible. The problem is less the lack of a course called "Theology of Women" or even "Women in Theology," and more the total absence of a single seminar on a female theologian. Particularly in survey courses, the descriptions of which contain long lists of more or less obscure male thinkers, why is there nothing on the women martyrs, mystics, writers, preachers, and reformers?

Perhaps the most bizarre result of the gendering of theological education is that it is possible to take master's level courses in homemaking at SWBTS, including one that advertises itself as an "intensive examination of the philosophic and personal aspects related to the professional Homemaking Specialist."[47] I admit I have no idea what a "professional Homemaking Specialist" is (a homemaker? a teacher of homemaking?), but my suspicion is that this is the result of a doomed desire to prove that "separate but equal" is a tenable way forward for graduate theological education. Homemaking is a worthwhile pursuit, but taking tuition money for graduate credit in its theoretical basis seems misleading, if not exploitative.

Why Do SBC Seminaries Have so Many Courses on Women?

SBC seminaries certainly have the most courses on women and for women. However, where "women" courses at my own school usually have to do with women thinkers, "women" courses at SBC schools, and many of those I counted elsewhere, have to do with *how* to be a woman. Even the "Feminist Theology" class at SWBTS puts "biblical feminism" in quotes in the course description and mentions goddess worship as a major issue at play. The attitude is anxious and hortatory, devoting an enormous amount of energy to how women ought to behave and view themselves. Feminism is considered ruinous, and therefore women being educated for theological reasoning at the same level as men is dangerous. "Women's studies," contrary to the SBC's revisionist take on the subject, is not a haphazard collection of every field's dispatch to women, rather it is an interdisciplinary endeavor in which *women* interact with many fields. Yet since SBC faculty must affirm complementarianism, other viewpoints are suppressed and theology about women is necessarily didactic. At the graduate level, this is inappropriate.

The situation is slightly different in practical departments, where many courses concern how to minister to women. This is useful, though it is interesting that the same concern is not shown for men—women seem to be a divergence from the male norm covered by "general" classes. Even in practical courses, however, ministers are being educated toward essentialist assumptions about what women need or how they work. How is "Creative Writing for Women" different from creative writing for men? This and other classes, like "Evangelism for Women," also imply that there are certain things covered in general classes that women are not allowed to do, or perhaps that men do not want to be bothered sharing "serious" classes with women.

Dearth of History

At almost every school, history plays a small role in the curriculum. Lutheran and Anglican schools are the exception; at both LCMS seminaries and Nashotah House history makes up about a quarter of the course catalog. However, both Lutheran schools list history as Historical Theology, as do RTS and MBTS. For the most part, courses in these departments seem to lean in the historical direction, rather than the theological. However, this exposes some lack of interest in history as a discipline that is matched at other schools. Across all fifteen seminaries, history makes up only 10% of the course content, just over half the figure for theology and less than a fourth of that for practical courses. Women's history makes up only 0.28% of all courses. *Women's* history is far more varied and interesting than are the roles women are "supposed" to play. Yet without courses on it or content within survey courses, the men who will produce the next generation of complementarian theology and practice are never asked to interact with the ways in which women have always stepped outside of those roles.

Conclusion

These data expose a number of problems. First, women are a special interest topic, unnecessary to a pastor's education. Those courses that do concern women are largely practical; having to do with how to be a woman, what to do with women, and how women differ from men. Being a woman seems to be a predicament, one that diverges from the norm and requires special instructions. This extends to marriage, which is treated as a relationship for men but a career for women. Second, these seminaries are either unaware of or unwilling to bother with women's *work* in theology, history, and biblical studies, and in some cases ban them from training for or engaging in it. Third, women professors, present in very small numbers, are often not required to have the same credentials as men, even as qualified candidates are turned away from those departments that make up schools' core curricula. Women teach courses to other women that are supposedly important enough to confer graduate credit, yet the administration cannot be bothered to find qualified instructors. Finally, women matter academically only as they define a role distinct from men. This relationship is always presented as a binary, in which women flourish in some sort of "opposite" sphere. However, *norm* and *special interest divergence* do not form a binary. This relationship is rather like that between a body and its orbiting object. The *role* of "woman" is what is interesting, one that serves the interests of the normative male by truncating the development of the person who occupies it. Thus, we have dozens of seminary courses on how to be a woman, what is proper to women, or how women should relate to men, and none on what women have discovered about God.

Given complementarians' universally weak explanations of Deborah's role in biblical history, I do not expect that just knowing women's history would cause an overnight shift in attitudes toward women's ministry. However, since this is rarely, if ever, addressed in education, the myth continues that complementarianism is "traditional." What is in fact traditional is a philosophical system of rank patriarchy, and a long line of women who successfully acted in opposition to it for the good of church and society. The complementarian desire to promote ontological equality with teleological inequality is a new quest, one that seeks to preserve the conclusions of the patriarchal argument without the propositions on which they rest. The ontological inequality of men and women has always been a deep foundation of the theological systems of the church, arising not from the Bible but from philosophy. It is only very recently that anyone challenged this assumption, but both complementarians and egalitarians claim to oppose it. The difference is that egalitarians have followed equality to its logical end, while complementarians have not.

As a result, nearly forty years from the inception of this debate, we see complementarians begin to shift in a more philosophically patriarchal direction, parsing what is minimally necessary and sufficient for the condition "ontological equality with men" while allowing gendered binaries and hierarchy to pervade theology and hermeneutics at every level. It is this confusion that allows for the theologically bankrupt (and historically ignorant) doctrine of the eternal (functional) subordination of the Son, as a temporary stopper for the hole in the logic. High-profile figures promote "masculine Christianity,"[48] and recent theology has gone so far as to say that complementarianism and the gospel "are one,"[49] both exposing not just the idolatry of gender, but a desperation to solve the unsolvable problem of complementarianism by doubling down on its position as a constituent pillar of orthodoxy. I suspect that within a few generations, as this untenable position continues to produce unstable, indefensible practice, those complementarians who have rested their hope in gender hierarchy will head for the truly "traditional" position of total philosophical patriarchy, while the others will move toward egalitarianism.

Welcoming women into theological education does not mean offering classes on how to support "real" theologians. Theology is a personal discipline, success in which comes from living, moving, and having one's being in the subject of study. The male claim to objectivity is a mirage. All theology is imprecise; there is no absolute knowledge of the infinite God who first made himself known by his freedom and lack of reference to humankind, then by his unsearchable incarnation, then by his individual indwelling of each one of us. We are his, not the other way around. Since God's Spirit is in women as well as men, there is no privileged access to truth that comes with being male, and the enormous variation in theological viewpoints, even among men who could sign the Chicago Statement on Inerrancy, should make this obvious. Mere belief in biblical authority does not guarantee truth or unity because the Bible is not God. Rather, the Holy Spirit makes known what he will make known to whom he will make it known, and what is made known is never the full truth about God. Nor is any person infallibly the mouthpiece of the Holy Spirit. The whole church contributes to this work of love that has no goal but love and no end but love. To ignore women's contributions to this work is to fail in this work, because it is to claim that the work belongs to human beings.

Notes

1. Beth Allison Barr, "Is There Hope for Evangelical Women?" *The Anxious Bench* (blog), May 16, 2018, accessed August 29, 2018. http://www.patheos.com/blogs/anxiousbench/2018/05/is-there-hope-for-evangelical-women-beth-moore-paige-patterson/.

2. The books in question are *The Story of Christianity*, Volume I by Justo Gonzalez and *Readings in the History of Christian Theology* by William C. Placher.

3. A brief summary of this research will appear in a chapter by Mimi Haddad in *Discovering Biblical Equality*, 3rd edition (forthcoming).

4. Data from the Survey of Doctorate Recipients (all fields) reported by Nicholas H. Wolfinger, "For Female Scientists, There's No Good Time to Have Children," *The Atlantic*, last modified July 29, 2013, accessed August 24, 2018, https://www.theatlantic.com/sexes/archive/2013/07/for-female-scientists-theres-no-good-time-to-have-children/278165/.

5. All data collected from conference programs and journals. These are available online at www.etsjets.org.

6. Westminster Theological Seminary, *2018–2019 Academic Catalog*, July 9, 2018, https://www.wts.edu/wp-content/uploads/2018/07/2018-2019-Catalog-v.3.pdf.

7. Reformed Theological Seminary, *Catalog: 2017–2019*, accessed August 24, 2018, https://www.rts.edu/Site/Academics/Courses/Catalogs/RTS-Catalog-2017-19.pdf.

8. "Faculty," Covenant Theological Seminary, accessed August 24, 2018. https://www.covenantseminary.edu/academics/faculty/.

9. Bob Jones University, *Seminary & Graduate Catalog: 17–18*, accessed August 24, 2018, https://www.bju.edu/academics/resources-support/catalogs/grad-catalog-2017.pdf.

10. Bethlehem College and Seminary, *2017–2018 Academic Catalog*, accessed August 24, 2018, http://2uxt2berb3uz5oi1iq6uzjv0-wpengine.netdna-ssl.com/wp-content/uploads/2017/11/AcademicCatalog2017-18-v4.pdf. The female non-adjunct faculty member is the librarian; the two adjuncts teach undergraduates in non-theological fields.

11. Trinity School for Ministry, *Academic Catalog & Student Handbook 2017–2018*, accessed August 24, 2018, https://www.tsm.edu/wp-content/uploads/2017/08/2017-2018-Academic-Catalog-Online.pdf.

12. Nashotah House Theological Seminary, *Academic Catalog 2017–2018*, accessed August 24, 2018, https://www.nashotah.edu/sites/default/files/academics/5%20-%202017-2018%20Academic%20Catalog.pdf.

13. Concordia Seminary, St. Louis, *Academic Catalog 2018–2019*, accessed August 24, 2018, https://www.csl.edu/files/AcademicCatalog2018-19.pdf.

14. Concordia Theological Seminary–Fort Wayne, *2017–2018 Academic Catalog*, accessed August 24, 2018, https://www.ctsfw.edu/wp-content/uploads/2018/03/Academic-Catalog-2017-18.pdf.

15. Southern Baptist Theological Seminary, *2017–2018 Academic Catalog*, accessed August 24, 2018, http://www.sbts.edu/admissions/wp-content/uploads/sites/3/2017/09/AR-322-2017-Southern-Seminary-Academic-Catalog-2017-18-web-Sept2017.pdf.

16. "2018–2019 Academic Catalog," Southwestern Baptist Theological Seminary, accessed August 24, 2018. http://catalog.swbts.edu/.

17. "Academic Catalog 2018–2019," Southeastern Baptist Theological Seminary, accessed August 24, 2018. http://catalog.sebts.edu/index.php.

18. Midwestern Baptist Theological Seminary, 2017–2018 Academic Catalog, accessed August 24, 2018, https://www.mbts.edu/downloads/_current_students/seminary_catalog_17-18.pdf.

19. New Orleans Baptist Theological Seminary, *2018–19 Graduate Catalog*, accessed August 24, 2018, http://www.nobts.edu/_resources/pdf/academics/GraduateCatalog.pdf.

20. Gateway Seminary, *2018–2019 Academic Catalog*, accessed August 24, 2018, https://07fbcb0072181791bed1-63fc6f11b2ad7905e74d76d8e23a9e05.ssl.cf2.rackcdn.com/uploaded/2/0e7342541_1533662677_2018-2019-academic-catalog.pdf.

21. Most recent available data published by Association of Theological Schools, "Table 3.1-A Number of Full-Time Faculty by Race/Ethnicity, Rank, and Gender – All Schools" in "2017–2018 Annual Data Tables," accessed August 24, 2018, https://

www.ats.edu/uploads/resources/institutional-data/annual-data-tables/2017-2018-annual-data-tables.pdf.

22. Data for Table 3 is available in each respective catalog; see notes on Table 2.

23. Covenant Theological Seminary, *Course Offerings 2017–2018 Academic Year*, accessed August 24, 2018, https://www.covenantseminary.edu/wp-content/uploads/2017/04/Course-Offerings-2017-2018-v1A.pdf.

24. Data for Table 4 is counted from each respective catalog; see notes on Table 2 and Table 3.

25. Southern Baptist Theological Seminary lists history courses under Theology and Tradition; this department has been counted entirely as history.

26. Data for Table 5 is counted from each respective catalog; see notes on Table 2 and Table 3.

27. Data for Table 6 is counted from each respective catalog; see notes on Table 2 and Table 3

28. Trinity School for Ministry's "Modern Theology" class includes feminist theology on the syllabus.

29. Data for Table 7 is counted from each respective catalog; see notes on Table 2 and Table 3.

30. Presuming that "Judges-Esther" and "Joshua-Kings" contain significant material on Esther and Ruth.

31. Presuming that "Historical Books (Joshua-Esther)" contains significant material on Esther and Ruth.

32. This counts two courses, each offered separately for Hebrew and English exegesis.

33. Two courses; Hebrew and English exegesis.

34. Data for Table 8 is counted from each respective catalog; see notes on Table 2 and Table 3.

35. These courses are also limited to women students. Among other history courses, "Formative Influences in American Christianity" discusses "feminism and feminization" of the church in what appears to be a negative light, and the Renaissance and Reformation course assigns the writings of Marguerite of Navarre.

36. A few women's history courses are offered in SWBTS's Women's Studies department, which is part of a program that confers certificates and offers master's and doctoral concentrations. See Discussion for more on this.

37. Data for Table 9 is counted from each respective catalog; see notes on Table 2 and Table 3.

38. For a revealing discussion of how this affects women's experiences of ETS membership and participation, see Emily Zimbrick-Rogers, "'A Question Mark Over My Head': Experiences of Women ETS Members at the 2014 ETS Annual Meeting," *A Question Mark Over My Head: A Special Edition Journal of Christians for Biblical*

Equality, 2015. https://www.cbeinternational.org/sites/default/files/A%20Question%20Mark%20Over%20My%20Head.pdf.

39. Westminster Theological Seminary, *2018–2019 Academic Catalog*.

40. "About," Bethlehem College and Seminary, accessed August 27, 2018. https://bcsmn.edu/about/#mission.

41. Association of Theological Schools, "Table 2.18-A Head Count Completions by Degree Program, Race or Ethnic Group, and Gender, Fall 2017" in "2017–2018 Annual Data Tables," accessed August 24, 2018, https://www.ats.edu/uploads/resources/institutional-data/annual-data-tables/2017-2018-annual-data-tables.pdf.

42. Reformed Theological Seminary, "General Information: Professor Ordination," in *Catalog: 2017–2019*.

43. "About Mary" Mary Kassian, accessed August 27, 2018. https://www.marykassian.com/about/. I was unable to find a biographical page for Kassian on the seminary's website.

44. This idea comes from Genesis 2 and 1 Corinthians 11. It is beyond my purposes here to dispute complementarian interpretations of these passages. However, it is worth noting that Paul contradicts himself in 1 Cor 11:8-9 and 12. "For a man is not ἐκ a woman…for a man was not created διὰ the woman…" (8-9); "For just as the woman is ἐκ the man, so also the man διὰ the woman" (12). This obvious parallel is obscured in almost all translations in order to avoid a contradiction, but it is more likely we who are confused than Paul.

45. *Ask Pastor John*, episode 1149, "Is There a Place for Female Professors at Seminary?" John Piper, posted January 2, 2018, on *Desiring God* (blog), https://www.desiringgod.org/interviews/is-there-a-place-for-female-professors-at-seminary.

46. Westminster Theological Seminary, 2018-2019 Academic Catalog, 6.

47. "School of Church and Family Ministries," Southwestern Baptist Theological Seminary, accessed August 28, 2018. http://catalog.swbts.edu/course-descriptions/school-of-church-and-family-ministries/.

48. John Piper, "The Frank and Manly Mr. Ryle: The Value of a Masculine Ministry," (sermon, "Desiring God 2012 Conference for Pastors," Minneapolis, MN, January 2012).

49. Owen Strachan and Gavin Peacock, *The Grand Design* (Tain, UK: Christian Focus, 2016), 166.

Chesna Hinkley will graduate from Princeton Theological Seminary in 2019 with an MDiv and a Certificate in Theology, Women, and Gender. She holds a BS in neuroscience from the University of Pittsburgh, where she was the first (but not last) woman to preach at her church. Chesna is currently an intern at Madison Avenue Presbyterian Church in New York City.

Write for CBE
Your voice matters. Let us amplify it.

CBE is always looking for talented writers to contribute to our print and digital platforms. From academic research to poetry to blog posts, we welcome your submissions.

Learn more at cbe.today/write

Fight Gender-Based Violence in Africa

CBE acts where global development and Christian belief intersect. Gender equality is not attainable without addressing underlying cultural and faith-based beliefs that devalue and disempower women and girls, making them vulnerable to abuse.

Help CBE collaborate with ministry leaders and other change agents in Africa to address gender power imbalances with culturally appropriate biblical resources.

Donate at cbe.today/africa

CBE Conferences

Learn. Network. Advocate.

CBE conferences bring together egalitarian leaders from around the world to tackle the most pressing issues related to gender and the Christian community.

Learn from leaders in the field. **Network** with fellow egalitarians. Get the tools to **advocate** in your context.

cbe.today/conference

cbeBookstore

Visit cbebookstore.com for the best resources on the Bible and gender, all reviewed and approved by CBE.

www.cbebookstore.com

Join the Movement

When your church or organization joins CBE as a member, it gets the tools it needs to advocate for biblical gender equality.

Visit cbe.today/orgsale to get 15–25% off a church/organization membership.

To learn more, visit cbe.today/orgmembers

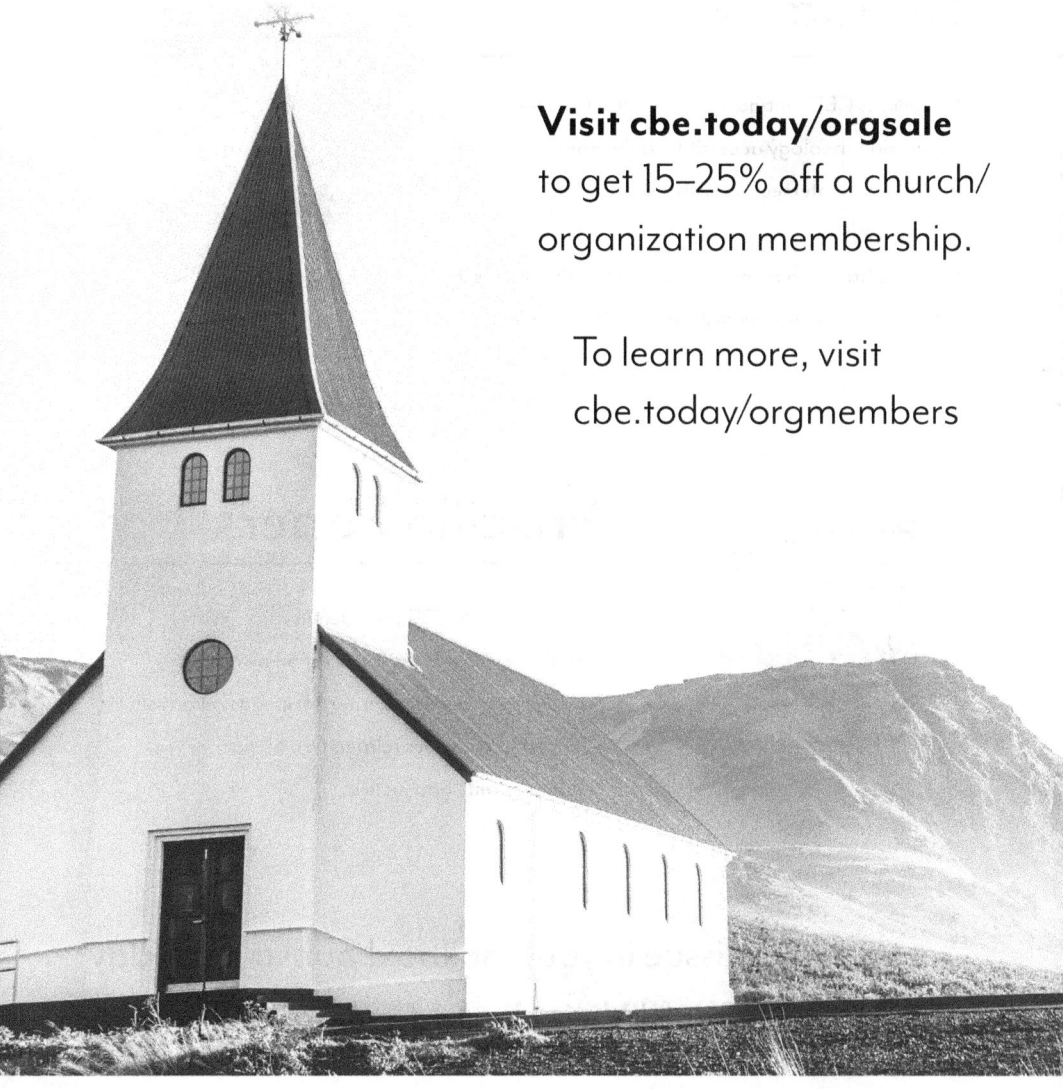

Subscribe to CBE's Award-winning Publications

Mutuality

Mutuality is CBE's magazine. Its goal is to make egalitarian theology accessible to the non-scholar and to explore its intersection with everyday life.

Mutuality has been recognized with 21 Higher Goals in Christian Journalism awards from the Evangelical Press Association.

Priscilla Papers

Priscilla Papers is CBE's academic voice. Winner of 18 Evangelical Press Association awards, it provides peer-reviewed, interdisciplinary evangelical scholarship on topics related to a biblical view of gender equality and justice.

Get every new issue in your mailbox! Subscribe today and get 15–25% off! **Visit cbe.today/subscriptionsale.**

Help Churches End Abuse

In the US, 1 in 3 women are victims of physical violence by an intimate partner, and studies show abuse is as common in the church as anywhere else.

CBE is developing a Bible-based resource to help church leaders and educators create communities that prevent abuse and promote the flourishing of women as equals beside men.

Help church leaders learn how to create communities that practice biblical gender equality visibly and intentionally.

Give at cbe.today/stopabuse

KEVIN GILES

Complementarian Theology in Crisis

In June 2016, professor Carl Trueman, of Westminster Theological Seminary, a complementarian, wrote:

> Complementarianism as currently constructed would seem to be now in crisis. But this is a crisis of its own making—the direct result of the incorrect historical and theological arguments upon which the foremost advocates of the movement have chosen to build their case and which cannot actually bear the weight being placed upon them.[1]

Many other leading complementarians in the last two years have reached much the same conclusion.[2] The sharpest critics of the complementarian position are now within the complementarian camp. The crisis began when in 2016 several complementarian theologians denounced as "heresy" and "Arian" the belief in hierarchically ordered Trinity, popularized by the *de facto* leaders of the complementarian movement, Wayne Grudem and Bruce Ware.[3] Then came the #MeToo and #ChurchToo movements which led to numerous evangelical women coming forward to say they had been abused by evangelical men who believed in male headship.[4] This made many complementarians realize that their headship teaching could, and often did, have harmful consequences for women. It could be toxic for them. What has not been publicly acknowledged so far by complementarians is the fact that in all the major exegetical debates they have had with evangelical egalitarians they have lost completely.[5] It is now obvious that the so-called "biblical argument" for male headship has no textual support, and that the complementarian appeal to the Bible can only persuade ill-informed anxious young men and already convinced complementarians.

The Invention of the Complementarian Position

In 1977, in the face of the growing impact of feminism on society and the church, George Knight III published his seminal work on the now-called "complementarian" view on gender, *New Testament Teaching on the Role Relationship of Men and Women*.[6] He claimed that he was enunciating the historical or traditional view of the man-woman relationship, and this is true to some degree, but how he worded and formulated his case was entirely novel. He rejected the historic way of speaking of men as "superior" and women as "inferior," replacing this with "role differences." Men and women are "equal" but men's "role" is to rule, and women's to obey. These differing "roles," he said, were given in creation before the fall and thus are transcultural and trans-temporal. He also introduced the novel idea that the hierarchical ordering of the sexes was grounded in the eternal triune life of God. This he claimed was what Paul clearly taught in 1 Corinthians 11:3: an "authority relationships that God has established between the Father and the Son, the Son and man, and man and woman."[7] Just as the Father is "head-over" the Son so men are "head-over" women. Knight openly admitted that this hierarchical ordering of the divine persons has "ontological" implications.[8]

The most creative and significant element in Knight's novel case for the permanent subordination of women and the eternal subordination of the Son was his introduction of the word "role." In everyday usage and in sociological texts, a "role" speaks of routine behavior or acts that can change over time and differ from culture to culture. Without out ever telling his readers, Knight used the word "role" in a totally different sense, found in no dictionary. For him, and every complementarian who has followed him, a "role" speaks of what identifies one as a man or a woman. In creation God gave to man the ruling "role" and women the obeying "role." In other words, Knight used the word "role" to speak of *fixed power relations given at birth based on gender*. This was a brilliant ploy, enabling him and all the complementarians who followed to speak of the permanent subordination of women in fine sounding terms that obfuscated what was actually being argued. They could assert that men and women are "equal" yet role differentiated.

But Knight's creative genius went further than this. He associated together a number of disparate texts, Genesis 2, 1 Corinthians 11:3–16, 14:33–34, Ephesians 5:22–33, and most importantly, 1 Timothy 2:11–14 into a theological construct. These texts, he argued, all spoke of the creation-given subordination of women and thus what they say is binding on the church for all times. Taken together these texts and their supposed creation grounding convinced many that Scripture permanently subordinated women to men. It is "what the Bible teaches."

In this book, Knight enunciated for the first time, almost word for word as it is today, "the complementarian position."

What is surprising is how many evangelicals uncritically embraced this novel teaching. They enthusiastically accepted Knights use of the term "role," taken from the theater and humanistic sociology, not the Bible, as a good-sounding way to speak of the permanent subordination of women and as an aid to the interpretation of their key texts. And they also accepted without dissent his hierarchically ordered Trinity that was a denial of historic orthodoxy.

The Trinity Argument

It is important to note that following Knight's book, his "Trinity argument" got little attention.[9] I took part in many forums, verbal and written, on the status and ministry of women in the 1980s, and the Trinity hardly got a mention. What was central to the debate in these years was the interpretation of a limited number of texts that Knight had highlighted, especially 1 Tim 2:11–14. This observation is shown to be true by the absence of any mention of the Trinity in the Danvers Statement of 1987, which outlined definitively what is now called the "complementarian" position.

It was with the publication of Wayne Grudem's *Systematic Theology*[10] in 1994 that the Trinity argument first became integral to the complementarian position. It was apparent by then that the proof-text theology Knight had invented could convince no evangelical biblical scholar who was not an already-convinced complementarian. More theological firepower was needed. Grudem gives a full chapter to the doctrine of the Trinity in which he argues for the eternal subordination of the Son, claiming this is clearly taught in Scripture and is what the church has always believed.[11] It is orthodoxy.

He makes this the ultimate basis for the permanent subordination of women. He argues that the hierarchical ordering of the sexes on earth is predicated on the hierarchical ordering of the divine three persons in eternity.[12] Breaking with Knight, however, he argues that the *eternal subordination* of the Son in "role" does not have ontological implications (that is, his *eternal* role subordination does not necessarily imply that he is subordinated in his person—less than the Father in "essence/being/substance," to use the technical terms—something the creeds and confessions of the church exclude). All complementarians followed him in this argument until 2016, when they capitulated, admitting that to *eternally* subordinate the Son must have ontological implications (meaning it implies what the creeds and confessions of the church deem heresy).[13]

Grudem quotes many texts in support of "the Trinity argument," most of them highlighted by Arius, that may imply or do speak of the subordination of the Son,[14] and he appeals to 2 Corinthians 1:3 to establish a connection between the hierarchical ordering of the Father and the Son and men and women, but his primary argument for this ordering is found in the revealed titles, "the Father" and "the Son." These are taken literally; the Father is a real father and the Son a real son. Fathers rule over sons and sons obey. He says,

> The Father and the Son relate to one another as a father and a son relate to one another in a human family; the Father directs and has authority over

> the Son, and the son obeys and is responsive to the directions of the father. The Holy Spirit is obedient to the directives of both the Father and the Son.[15]

And then pushing the human analogy even further he says,

> The gift of children within a marriage, coming from both the father and the mother, and subject to the authority of the father and the mother, is analogous to the relationship of the Holy Spirit to the Father and the Son in the Trinity.[16]

Grudem's analogical argument seemed compelling for evangelicals who were ill-informed on the doctrine of the Trinity, had little interest in the creeds and confessions of the church, and had no understanding of the nature of human words used of God. The Son is like a human son and thus must obey his father. From this point on the Trinity argument became central to the complementarian case. Books and articles in support flooded the evangelical world. Possibly the most telling book in support was Bruce Ware's *Father, Son and Holy Spirit: Relationships, Roles, and Relevance*.[17]

It is surprising that most evangelicals embraced uncritically this analogically-predicated theology. Evangelicals should always predicate our theology in Scripture, never on parallels with fallen human existence and relationships. In the New Testament, the Father-Son relationship is spoken of in terms of love, intimacy, and unity, never in terms of differing authority. When it comes to the Son, he is depicted as the Son of the King of Kings who will rule for ever and ever (2 Sam 7:2–4; Is 9:7; Lk 1:33; 2 Peter 1:11; Rev 7:10–12; 11:15; c.f. Eph 1:20). What is more, to argue by way of human analogy that the Son of God is eternally subordinated in authority to the Father is a denial of the primary Christian confession, "Jesus is Lord."

The Biblical Argument

Genesis 1–3

Now we turn to the "biblical argument" for the permanent subordination of women, invented in its contemporary form by George Knight. This is based on the belief that God set the man over the woman before the fall. Male "headship" is the creational ideal; it is not a cultural phenomenon.

In support of the premise that the man ruled over the woman before the fall, complementarians characteristically argue that:

1. The man was created first and this means he is "first," the leader.
2. God created woman as man's "helper" (i.e. a subordinate).
3. Woman was made from and for man, not vice versa.
4. God gave the command not to eat of the tree of the knowledge of good and evil to Adam, not to Eve, thereby making it clear that he was in charge in the Garden.
5. Adam named the animals and Eve. Naming implies "authority over."
6. Eve was the first to be deceived by the serpent/devil. This demonstrates that women are more prone to sin and deception, and thus need the leadership of men.
7. After Adam and Eve had both sinned, God spoke first to Adam, again showing that he had put him in charge.

If these are true, then the punishment God gives to the woman for her sin, namely that she will desire her husband but he will rule over her (Gen 3:16), introduces *nothing* new. Adam ruled over Eve before the fall.

These arguments have a long history. They were developed in a patriarchal culture where men ruled over women and no one questioned male supremacy. The problem for contemporary complementarians is that virtually no modern scholarly commentary of Genesis—Protestant or Catholic—endorses these arguments. The vast majority of scholars reject all of them. The Roman Catholic Church in a binding encyclical rejects every one, insisting that Genesis chapters 1–3 speak of "the essential equality of the sexes," and makes the fall the basis for the rule of the man over the woman.[18]

All seven arguments are inferences. They are not exegesis but speculation. I now critically evaluate these seven proofs for the pre-fall subordination of women.

1. *The man was created first and this means he is "first," the leader.* This argument has no force. First, what is created second is often better or

more preeminent than what is created prior. In Genesis 1, man and woman were created last, but they rule supreme. John the Baptist came first, Jesus second, but Jesus is preeminent. Second, the argument runs counter to what the dramatic narrative implies. Adam appears "first" to make the point that man alone is incomplete, help-less, not to indicate he rules supreme or is complete in himself. Paul once notes the fact that Adam in Genesis 2 is created first (1 Tim 2:13). He does so to back up his prohibition that *a* woman should not teach *a* man in a domineering (in Greek, *authentein*) way. In other words, women in Ephesus should not put themselves "first."

2. *God created woman as man's "helper" (i.e. a subordinate).* The Hebrew word *ezer* ("helper") is used twenty-one times in the Old Testament, fifteen times of God, the sovereign helper of Israel. Nowhere is it used of a subordinate helper. We thus must ask; what sort of helper does God provide for Adam? The text itself tells us that "the helper" is neither a superior nor a subordinate. The Hebrew word *kenegdo* that qualifies *ezer* defines the helper as one corresponding to him—literally "according to, or the opposite of."[19] The two words taken together thus speak of a fitting partner or companion for Adam.[20]

3. *Woman was made from and for the man, not vice versa.* In Genesis 2, woman is made for man, because alone he is help-less, incomplete, and from man to highlight that woman is made of the same stuff as man. She is just like him yet she is woman and he is man. In neither case do these relationships imply subordination. In 1 Corinthians 11:8–9, Paul agrees that woman came "from" and was made "for" man in creation, but then says "nevertheless" "in the Lord" (in the new creation) man and woman are dependent on one another and he adds, man now comes "from" woman. In this argument, Paul first differentiates the two sexes by these two prepositions and then excludes the idea that differentiation implies the subordination of the woman.

4. *God gave the command not to eat of the tree of the knowledge of good and evil to Adam, not to Eve, thereby making it clear that he was in charge in the Garden.* Yes, God gave the command to Adam, but Eve

did not exist at that time and later it is said the command was given to her as well (Gen 3:1).

5. *Adam named the animals and Eve. Naming implies "authority over."* This scene in the narrative is given to make the point that no animal was a suitable partner/companion for Adam, not to teach that Adam had an authority denied to woman. In any case, naming does not imply authority over but rather differentiation. To name someone John means they are not Harry. To name an elephant an elephant means it is not a lion. What is more, if naming implies male rule over and excludes women ruling then it directly contradicts Genesis 1:28 where God appoints the man and the woman to rule over the animals. In Genesis 2:23 the man does not name the woman. He simply recognizes she is other than him, a woman. After the fall, Adam names Eve (Gen 3:20).

6. *Eve was the first to be deceived by the serpent/devil. This demonstrates that women are more prone to sin and deception, and thus need the leadership of men.* Yes, the Serpent spoke with Eve and she first sinned but there are other possible inferences that can be drawn from these details in the narrative. More plausible than the one given by complementarians is that the Serpent reasoned, "If I can lead the woman into sin, the man will be a push over." This was the case. We should also note that the author of Genesis says Adam was "with her" when she sinned (Gen 3:6). They thus sinned conjointly. In 1 Tim 2:14 Paul mentions the deception of Eve, as a warning to the women who have been "deceived" in Ephesians and are teaching in an *authentein*/dominating way.

7. *After Adam and Eve both sinned, God spoke first to Adam, again showing that he had put him in charge.* In each of the seven scenes in Genesis 2–3, one actor is first. No one suggests this implies deep theology in each case. This phenomenon is best explained as stylistic. We should therefore not without any basis give weight to God addressing Adam first in this scene. In any case in this scene Adam is not depicted as the

strong leader who is in charge, but rather as a weak man who blames his wife for his sin (Gen 3:12).

What must be acknowledged is that all these arguments are special pleading, not exegesis. They are a reading into the text what men in the past and some men today want to believe. In Genesis 1:27–28 in totally unambiguous language, man and woman are alike made in the image of God, together, side by side, they are given rule over creation (not one over the other), and to both of them is given the family mandate. Differing "roles" for men and women—in either the sociological sense or in Knight's sense—are never implied or suggested.

So compelling is this interpretation of Genesis 1:27–28 that the dogmatic complementarians, Andreas and Margaret Köstenberger, in their 2014 book, *God's Design for Men and Women*, admit that according to Genesis chapter 1, "Ruling the earth is a joint function of the man and the woman. Humanity is conceived as plurality."[21] Despite this admission, they then argue that Genesis chapter 2 teaches the subordination of women and give the seven arguments just listed. In doing so, they not only set Genesis 1 and 2 in conflict but also ignore the fact that their interpretation has no scholarly support.

What we should believe, following almost all contemporary scholarly commentators, is that Genesis chapters 1 and 2 make basically the same points about man and woman in different literary genres. These chapters speak of the essential equality of the two sexes, their differentiation and complementarity, their joint dominion over creation, and that the rule of the man over the woman is entirely a consequence of the fall—not the creation ideal.

If in fact Genesis chapters 1–3 do not make male "headship" the creational ideal but rather a consequence of sin, then the complementarian view is without a theological foundation and it must be rejected.

The Rest of the Old Testament

Most of the Old Testament reflects fallen existence where the man rules over the woman but God in his wisdom makes it clear that the subordination of women is not a reflection of his perfect will. He thus includes the story of Deborah, among others. Deborah is a married woman whom God raises up to be a judge and prophet set over his people Israel. (Judges 4 and 5). She cannot be explained away as all complementarians want to do. This story is included in our Bibles as a denial of the idea that the subordination of women is the God-given ideal and that God does not endorse the leadership of women. Deborah is a leader of God's people, a judge or ruler and prophet like the men so designated. All scholarly commentators on the book of Judges acknowledge this fact.

Deborah is not the only woman called a prophet in Scripture. Miriam (Ex 15:21–12), Huldah (2 Kings 22:14), Noadiah (Neh 6:14), the wife of Isaiah (Isa 8:3), Anna (Lk 2:36), and other women who are unnamed are said to prophesy.[22] A prophet is raised up by God as his spokesperson. He or she is a leader among God's people. A prophet could call to account a king or priest. Prophets among other things were teachers of God's people. They were forthtellers more than foretellers.

Jesus

In complementarian writings, Jesus' teaching and example in regard to women is generally ignored; only the fact that he appointed twelve male apostles is stressed.[23] This is supposed to indicate that male leadership is a creation-given principle that Jesus endorsed. This omission of the Gospel accounts of Jesus' interactions with women by those claiming to be giving "what the Bible teaches" on women is unpardonable. Scholarly studies on Jesus and women are united in concluding that his stance on women was revolutionary and counter-cultural. He related to women in the same way as he related to men. He said not one word in support of male headship and much to the contrary.

It is a *fact* of history that Jesus chose twelve men to be his apostles. It is an *inference* that this indicates the principle of male leadership. This inference is not supported by anything Jesus said or did. Other inferences are much more plausible. For instance, he likely chose twelve men because leadership in ancient Israel was customarily given by men and because women were not regarded as trustworthy factual witness by the Jews—and the Twelve were primarily witnesses of Jesus' ministry, death, and resurrection (Acts 1:21–22). Furthermore, it seems the number *twelve* was what was most significant. In choosing twelve men,

Jesus was indicating that his followers were the new Israel. Lastly, I mention that Luke also insists that the seven table waiters mentioned in Acts 6:1–6 must be men. To be consistent should not complementarians insist that all work in church kitchens be done by men? That they serve morning tea or coffee?

1 Corinthians 11:3–16

Paradoxically, this text is one of the most quoted in the complementarian case, despite being the clearest evidence that men and women *led* in prayer and prophecy in church in the apostolic age.[24] Charles Hodge says prayer and prophecy were "the two principal exercises in the public life of the early Christians."[25] Complementarians quote this text primarily because they interpret Paul to be saying God is "head over" the Son and men "head over women" (verse 3). This they insist is the force of the Greek word *kephalē* (head) whenever it is used in the New Testament. Are they right?

As in English, the Greek word literally refers to the top part of the body. Unlike in English, its metaphorical uses don't include "leader" but do include the top part, beginning, or source of something. Despite denials by complementarians. The verdict is now in: *kephalē* can mean "source," and in this context this is the most likely meaning.[26] The Father is the source of the Son in his eternal generation and Adam is the source of woman according to Genesis chapter 2, a fact Paul mentions in verses 8 and 12. Why would Paul first say men have authority over women and then endorse them leading in prayer and prophecy?

This affirmation of women leading in prophecy is hugely difficult for complementarians because in the Bible prophets are teachers of God's people. The Old Testament prophets were certainly teachers of God's people; Jesus is a prophet who teaches, and Luke speaks of prophets and teachers as one ministry (Acts 13:1). Paul says that when prophets prophesy they "build up, encourage and console" the assembled church (1 Cor 14:3) and their hearers "learn" (1 Cor 14:31), which is what happens when people teach. In Revelation 2:20 we read of Jezebel, "who calls herself a prophet and is teaching and beguiling my servants." In this verse a prophet, albeit a false prophet, is said to teach. In his important study on prophecy in the apostolic age, David Hill argues that prophecy is basically Spirit-inspired teaching.[27]

The passage certainly affirms male-female differentiation, but it says not one word on the subordination of women. Indeed, it is one of the clearest texts showing that women led and "preached" in church in the apostolic age.

1 Corinthians 14:33b–36

Complementarians next turn to 1 Corinthians 14:33b–36 where they find Paul saying, "Women should keep silent in the churches." They take Paul to be forbidding women speaking in church in any way that would question male headship. This is a very unlikely interpretation because in 1 Corinthians 11:3, as we have just seen, Paul allows that women can lead the church in prayer and prophecy. The explanation that Paul is forbidding women from asking disruptive questions in the little house churches is far more plausible. He says, if the women have anything to ask, "let them ask their husbands at home" (1 Cor 14:35).

But there is a bigger issue; it is highly likely that Paul did not write these words but that they were added by a later scribe. This has long been argued as a possibility, but in recent years Philip Payne has put forward compelling evidence for the omission of these verses in the earliest written manuscripts.[28] This means that there is a big question mark over the authenticity of this text. An agreed evangelical rule is that if there is serious doubt on the textual authenticity of any text in the Bible, it should not be quoted in support of any doctrine.

Ephesians 5:21–33

The principle of "male headship" is basic to the complementarian position. Nothing is more often mentioned. However, not once in the whole Bible do we find the term "headship" and only once do we find Paul saying, "the husband is the head of the wife" (Eph 5:23). In Ephesians 5:22–23 Paul says, "Wives submit to your husbands . . . for the husband is the head (*kephalē*) of the wife." *Like all verses in the Bible this verse must be read in context.* When it is, we discover that in Ephesians 5:21–33, Paul both affirms the cultural premise that the husband is the *paterfamilias* (father of the family)[29] *and* subverts any thought that this grants him privileges and power in relation to his wife.

He begins his discussion of Christian marriage in verse 21 with an exhortation, "Be subordinate to one another." This verse is transitional. It looks back to the string of imperatives that depend on the verb in the exhortation, "be filled with the Spirit" (5:18).[30] Paul believed that when Christians are filled with the Spirit they will sing and make melody, give thanks *and subordinate themselves to one another*. It looks forward by introducing what Paul goes on to say about marriage in verses 22–33.

Paul's exhortation, "Be subordinate (*hypotassesthai*) to one another out of fear/reverence for Christ" tells Spirit-filled believers how they are to relate to one another. He exhorts all Christians, men and women, as those set free by the Spirit, to defer to and humbly serve one another. Next, Paul exhorts Christian wives specifically to be subordinate to their husbands, an exhortation in sharp tension with the prior exhortation to mutual subordination and the following exhortations to husbands to give themselves in service and love for their wives. The reason a wife should submit to her husband, Paul says, is because "the husband is the *kephalē* / head of the wife" (v. 22). Because Paul has just instructed wives to be subordinate, and he does so again in verse 24, his first readers would have taken the word kephalē to be speaking of the husband's precedence as the *paterfamilias*, the master of the extended household, because this was their cultural understanding of the position of the husband in the marriage. In speaking of the man as the *kephalē* of his wife, Paul allowed his readers to think that he was simply reinforcing the cultural norms of that culture, what they already believed—men should have precedence and be privileged. It was only as they read on that they found he was giving entirely new content to what it means for the husband to be the *kephalē*.

In speaking of the husband as *the head* of the wife and in his exhortation to wives to be subordinate, Paul never mentions a supposed hierarchical, pre-fall creation order where the husband has authority over his wife. Nowhere in the New Testament do we find any hint of such an idea. What is reflected in verses 22–24 is the *cultural order* of that time, where men were set over women (and masters over slaves), an order Paul is trying to subvert but not explicitly reject. Behind this teaching lies Gen 3:16, which speaks of the post-fall situation where the man rules over the woman. In Ephesians 5:31, Paul does quote Genesis 2:24, not to establish the headship of the husband or the subordination of the wife, but rather to speak of the mysterious and profound oneness of man and woman in marriage.

Having given instruction to wives in three verses and having said nothing distinctively Christian or revolutionary, and having made no appeal to creation order, Paul devotes seven verses to husbands, asking of them things no one had ever asked of husbands before. In this section, we find much that is distinctively Christian and revolutionary. Paul asks husbands to love their wives "just as Christ loved the church and gave himself for her," and also, "as they love their own bodies." He does not use the Greek word *eros* (sexual love), or *philia* (brotherly/family love), but *agapē* (self-giving love). As far as we know, no one before Paul had used this word for the marriage relationship. *Agapē* is the noblest and loftiest word in the Greek language for love. We understand its meaning through the self-sacrifice of Christ who "loved (*agapaō*) the church and gave himself up for her" (v 25). What Paul says here subverts patriarchy; it envisages a marriage of two people of equal worth and dignity in which the man gives himself in sacrificial service for his wife.

Let me say again: Ephesians 5:21–33 does not make the rule of the husband over his wife the Christian position. The rule of the man over the women reflects the fall (Gen 3:16) and fallen existence. It is the well-nigh universal reality in this world. Rather, Paul in this profound text depicts Christian marriage as characterized by mutual subordination, where the man gives his life for his wife in costly service to the point of death. Professor Andrew Lincoln says that here Paul sees, "submission and love [*agape* love] as two sides of the same coin—selfless service of one's marriage partner." [31] It is thus best to understand Ephesians 5:21–33 as a foreshadowing of the fully equal marriage, which for the first time in history can now be realized and enjoyed.

1 Timothy 2:8–15

For the complementarian case, no text is more important than 1 Timothy 2:12–14. Complementarians take Paul to be clearly forbidding women from teaching or exercising pastoral authority in church, and they see him basing this prohibition in the hierarchical ordering of the sexes in creation before the fall. Thus, they read this one text as a binding rule for all time for all Christians. In reply I make the following points.

1. This prohibition is found in one of three related epistles (the Pastorals) in which false teaching is the primary concern (1 Tim 1:3–7, 19–20, 4:1–2, 16, 6:3–5, 2 Tim 2:14–19, 3:10–16, Tit 1:10–16, 2:1–2, 3:8–10). Writing to Titus in Crete where the false teachers were active, Paul tells his young deputy to "silence" the *men* who are "upsetting whole families" by teaching "what is not right to teach" (Tit 1:10–11). Writing to Timothy in Ephesus, Paul tells Timothy to silence the *women* who have been deceived and are teaching in an *authentein* way.[32] In Ephesus, Paul makes it plain the false male teachers were having a field day among the women. They had forbidden them to marry (1 Tim 4:3) and led some to "follow Satan," and some women were "going about from house to house" [house-church to house-church] . . . "saying what they ought not say" (1 Tim 5:13–15).

2. If this is a universal prohibition on women teaching/preaching then what Paul says here is in conflict with his own teachings elsewhere. He holds that the Spirit gives all ministries and the Spirit is given to men and women alike (1 Cor 12:4–31). He endorses women prophesying, and prophesying and teaching cannot be sharply divided. He almost certainly speaks of a woman apostle (Rom 16:7), and apostles definitely taught.[33]

3. The verb *authentein* almost certainly does not speak of the rightful authority that pastors exercise. Despite a huge effort, complementarian scholars have not been able to come up with one example where this word is used in a positive sense before Paul or in the next 100 years. The etymology of this word, its cognate forms, and its usage all indicate that it

speaks of self-appropriated and assertive authority. In this context is best translated "to usurp authority" or to "dominate." [34]

4. In 1 Timothy 2:8–15, the church as we know it today never comes into view. The context is the little house churches of the first century where everyone had an opportunity to minister (1 Cor 14:26) and to *teach* (Rom 15:4, Eph 5:19, Col 3:16). Speaking to such a church setting, Paul says, "I do not permit *a* woman to teach *a* man in an *authentein* way." Note carefully the singular. He forbids *a* woman dominating *a* man by the way she teaches in person to person interaction. Paul says nothing about preaching in a large public church gathering, whoever does it. We thus cannot simplistically apply what is *actually said* in this text to a very contrasting modern-day ecclesiastical setting.

5. Paul does not ground his prohibition in a supposed hierarchical ordering of the sexes before the fall. He forbids *a* woman teaching *a* man one-to-one in an *authentein* way. He uses two *ad hoc* arguments: Adam was created first (therefore you women should not put yourself first, claiming an authority not given to you) and like Eve, you women giving this false teaching are the ones who have been "deceived." Given this interpretation of 1 Timothy 2:13–14, Paul speaks not of a *hierarchical social order* given in creation before the fall, but rather of the *heresy-created disorder* in the church at Ephesus in the first century. If this is the case, then Paul's prohibition on women teaching and leading in church, however understood, is not universally binding.

In the case of 1 Timothy 2:12-14, complementarians have built far too much on one possible and unlikely interpretation of one text. I here recall what Oscar Cullman once said, "the fountainhead of all false biblical interpretation and all heresy is invariably the isolation and absolutizing of one single passage."

At this point, I conclude my critical assessment of the so-called "biblical case" for the permanent subordination of women. What we have discovered is that no text in the whole Bible grounds the subordination of women in creation before the fall. And, none of the texts that supposedly unilaterally subordinate women to men or demand their silence in church actually do so. The Bible makes the rule of the man over the woman entirely a consequence of the fall. It is not the God-given ideal.

The Beginning of the End

By the 1990s, complementarian theologians had realized that their "biblical argument" could not win the day. Informed evangelical scholars were not persuaded by their appeal to a limited number of texts or of their interpretation of them, and they were agreed that the use of the term "role" to interpret the contested texts only corrupted the exegetic process. It led to eisegesis—reading our agenda into the text.

Let me give two examples to illustrate this point. First, because of their fixation with "roles," complementarians insist that Adam and Eve's sin spoken of in Genesis 2–3 was that of "role reversal."[36] In fact, it was simply disobedience to the command of God. Second, whatever 1 Timothy 2:15 (women "will be saved through childbearing") means, it does not mean or imply, "women will be spiritually preserved if they devote themselves to their God-given role in the domestic and familial sphere"[37] as some complementarians teach. This is not exegesis. It is imaginative pious platitude.

I agree with Werner Neuer, a German Old Testament scholar of complementarian convictions. He speaks of the "inappropriateness of role theory" to interpret the Bible's teaching on the sexes, and concludes that, "in the cause of truth we [complementarians] should give up talking about the roles of the sexes."[38]

But not only has the "biblical argument" collapsed, so too has the "Trinity argument"—and complementarians now publicly admit this. It has been deemed by their own theologians as heretical.[39] Denny Burk, the president of the Council of Biblical Manhood and Womanhood, the flagship of the complementarian movement and a long-time supporter of the Trinity argument, openly says, "I now believe in the whole Nicene package," and he admits that the complementarian doctrine of the Trinity cannot be reconciled with it. For this reason, he says, I do not agree with "the specific formulations [of the doctrine of the Trinity] of Grudem and Ware," "my friends." Because he is now personally committed to the Nicene doctrine of the Trinity that excludes hierarchical ordering in the Trinity, he says, "I think it is good and right to leave behind the language of "subordination."[40] But worse was to follow.

The #MeToo Movement

Just as complementarians were accepting that they had to abandon the Trinity argument, an even more devastating assault began that exposed the awful practical consequences of complementarian theology. In the wake of the appalling revelations of Harvey Weinstein's predatory behavior towards women, first on the hashtag #MeToo, and then #ChurchToo, large numbers of evangelical women came forward to speak of their abuse by evangelical men.

This led to the Paige Patterson scandal.[41] In the late twentieth and early twenty-first century, Patterson was one of, if not the, most powerful and influential leader of the Southern Baptist denomination, the largest protestant denomination in the USA. He was a key player in the conservative victory over the moderates in Southern Baptist seminaries and a leading complementarian who helped draft the 1987 Danvers Statement.

The charges against him include that he had counselled evangelical woman to stay with their abusive husbands and taught that abuse was not a reason for divorce. He had publicly objectified a teenage girl by commenting on her good looks, and he criticized the appearance of many female theological students. In 2003, he had pressured a young Southeastern Baptist Theological Seminary student (where he was then President), named Megan Lively, not to report an incident of sexual assault to the police. In 2015, this time as President of Southwestern Baptist Theological Seminary, when another young female student reported that she had been raped, he insisted on speaking to the girl alone so that he, in his own words, "could break her down." And finally, he lied to the trustees of Southwestern about these matters.[42]

While abuse and the putting down of women do not occur solely in complementarian communities, complementarian teachings seem to encourage it and condone it. When egalitarians abuse or put down women, they cannot turn to their gender theology for justification or to excuse their behavior.

Evangelical Christians, many of them complementarians, cried out, "If this is how complementarianism works out in practice, can it be what the Bible teaches?" Possibly no one put this question more forcibly and painfully than Beth Moore, perhaps the best-known Southern Baptist. As a Southern

Baptist, she is of course not ordained and mainly speaks to women. She has long upheld complementarian teaching.

However, in the wake of the #MeToo movement and the Paige Patterson scandal, she broke ranks and wrote on May 3, 2018 an "Open Letter to My Brothers" [of complementarian conviction].[43] In this she says "she learned early to show constant pronounced deference—not just proper respect" to evangelical male leaders, to accept frequent unjustified criticism from them, and to be ignored and talked down to by these men. But in late 2016 when it emerged that many if not most the better-known complementarians' views of women "smacked of misogyny, objectification and astonishing disesteem" she spoke up. She writes,

> I came face to face with one of the most demoralizing realizations of my adult life: Scripture was not the reason for this colossal disregard and disrespect of women among these many men. It was only an excuse. Sin was the reason. Ungodliness.

At this point of time, she came to accept and acknowledge that "many women have experienced horrific abuses within the power structures of our [evangelical] world," and male evangelical leaders have been silent. She says,

> Many churches quick to teach submission are often slow to point out that women were also among the followers of Christ (Luke 8), that the first recorded word out of his resurrected mouth was "woman" (John 20:15) and that same woman was the first evangelist. These men love to turn to the Household codes in their sermons, where wives are told to be submissive, but are slow to also point out the numerous women with whom the apostle Paul served and for whom he possessed obvious esteem.

What is now demanded, she concludes, is a "roundtable discussion" where these issues can be faced and addressed honestly and openly.

Not unexpectedly, many read her words as a rejection and condemnation of complementarianism. Beth Allison Barr for one read it as a "recanting" of complementarianism, even though Moore does not explicitly say this. She does, however, apologize for "being part of the problem" created by complementarian teaching that demeans women and for her "cowardly" deference to its teachers. Furthermore, she reminds her readers of the frequent affirmations of women and their leadership in Scripture that complementarian theologians ignore or downplay.

Melanie McMaster, writing in the *Washington Post* in reference to Beth Moore's letter, says "The SBC leaders are well aware that they are [now] facing a continuing crisis over how women are treated [in their churches and seminaries]. Women such as Beth Moore have started to challenge men's abuse of power."[44] She then asks, could this be the beginning of the end of the complementarian ideology?

I think so. An appeal to the Bible that has awful consequences for millions of women, and demeans them by making them subordinate to men, must be wrong. Good theology leads to good outcomes. The gospel liberates and lifts up the downtrodden.

Where to Now?

The complementarian hold on American evangelicalism has been strong, but now it is on the ropes. Complementarianism is in "crisis," as Carl Trueman points out. Its biblical argument and its Trinity argument for the permanent subordination of women have collapsed, and it has been charged and found guilty of demeaning women and encouraging their abuse. Beth Moore has suggested a way forward, a "roundtable discussion" where evangelical supporters and critics of the complementarian position can listen to and learn from each other. To have this discussion, one thing is necessary. Complementarians must cease asserting that if anyone disagrees with what they say the Bible says, they have rejected the authority of Scripture. No evangelical egalitarian rejects the authority of Scripture. What we reject, for the reasons given in this essay, is the complementarian *interpretation* of a limited number of verses and the theological construct built on these texts. Let the discussion begin.

Notes

1. Carl Trueman, "Motivated by Feminism? A Response to a Recent Criticism," *Postcards from Palookaville* (blog), Mortification of Spin, Alliance of Confessing Evangelicals, June 7, 2016, http://www.alliancenet.org/mos/postcards-from-palookaville/motivated-by-feminism-a-response-to-a-recent-criticism#.W8TfuHtKiUm.
2. I document many examples later in this essay.
3. I will say more on this latter. See also Kevin Giles, *The Rise and Fall of the Complementarian Doctrine of the Trinity* (Eugene, OR: Cascade, 2017).
4. Again, I will document this assertion later in this essay.
5. As I will demonstrate later in this essay. See also Kevin Giles, *What the Bible Actually Teaches on Women: A Reply to the Köstenbergers* (Eugene, OR: Cascade, 2018).
6. George Knight III, *New Testament Teaching on the Role Relationship of Men and Women* (Grand Rapids: Baker, 1977).
7. Ibid, 57, See also 33.
8. Ibid, 56. Three times in the first paragraph on this page he admits this.
9. For what follows, see for greater detail and with full documentation Giles, *The Rise and Fall*.
10. Wayne Grudem, *Systematic Theology: An Introduction to Biblical Doctrine*, (Downers Grove: InterVarsity, 1994).
11. Ibid., 226–61.
12. Ibid., 459.
13. Giles, *The Rise and Fall*, 35–52
14. No one denies some texts do this. Nicene orthodoxy insists that such texts speak of the self–chosen subordination of the Son in his incarnation, as taught in Philippians 2:4–11.
15. Grudem, *Systematic Theology*, 249.
16. Ibid., 257.
17. Bruce Ware, *Father, Son and Holy Spirit: Relationships, Roles, and Relevance* (Wheaton: Crossway, 2005).
18. Pope John Paul II, *Apostolic Letter Mulieris Dignitatem of the Supreme Pontiff John Paul II On the Dignity and Vocation of Women On the Occasion of the Marian Year* (Boston: St. Paul Books & Media, 1988).
19. On the words used and their meaning see Philip Payne, *Man and Woman, One in Christ* (Grand Rapids: Zondervan, 2009), 44–45.
20. John Walton, *Genesis* (Grand Rapids: Zondervan, 2001), 177, thinks the best translation would be either "partner" or "counterpart."
21. Andreas and Margaret E. Köstenberger, *God's Design for Man and Woman:*

A Biblical–Theological Survey (Wheaton: Crossway, 2014), 30.

22. See further on prophets, Kevin Giles, *Patterns of Ministry among the First Christians*, second ed. (Eugene, OR: Cascade, 2017), 149–173.

23. An exception is found in Margaret E. Köstenberger's book, *Jesus and the Feminists: Who Do They Say He Is?* (Wheaton: Crossway, 2008). However, her pages on Jesus are not serious scholarship. In the end for her, Jesus is just a nice man who speaks respectfully to women.

24. I have a full chapter on prophets and prophesy in the Bible in my book, *Patterns of Ministry among the First Christians*, 149–173.

25. Charles Hodge, *A Commentary on the First Epistle to the Corinthians* (London: Banner of Truth, 1958), 208.

26. Payne, *Man and Woman*, 117–139 and Cynthia Westfall, *Paul and Gender: Reclaiming the Apostle's Vision for Men and Women in Christ* (Grand Rapids: Baker, 2016), 38–40, 80–89. No one has made an answer to Payne's overwhelming case.

27. David Hill, *New Testament Prophecy* (London: Marshall Morgan, and Scott, 1979).

28. See Payne, *Man and Woman*, 217–270 and more recently with added evidence, Payne, "Vaticanus Distigme-Obelos Symbols," *New Testament Studies*, 63.4 (2017), 604–625.

29. For more on this concept see Giles, *What the Bible Actually Teaches*, 108, 156–157.

30. The Köstenbergers agree. See *God's Design for Man and Woman*, 185.

31. Andrew Lincoln, *Ephesians: Word Biblical Commentary* (Dallas: Word, 1990), 393.

32. I will justify this reading of 1 Tim 2 immediately following.

33. I set out the compelling evidence for this in my, *What the Bible Actually Teaches*, 118–129, 144–151

34. Ibid., 144–151.

35. Oscar Cullman, *The State in the New Testament* (London: SCM, revised edition, 1963), 47.

36. As commonly asserted in complementarian literature. Knight, *New Testament Teaching*, 31, invented this idea.

37. Köstenberger, *God's Design*, 216

38. Werner Neuer, *Man and Woman in Christian Perspective* (London: Hodder and Stoughton, 1990) 30.

39. See also Giles, *The Rise and Fall*.

40. "My Take-Away's [sic] from the Trinity Debate," *Denny Burk* (blog), August 10, 2016, http://www.dennyburk.com/my-take-aways-from-the-trinity-debate/.

41. There are many accounts of this sad story on the internet. See for example, Kate Shellnutt, "Divorce after abuse: how Paige Patterson's Counsel Compares to

other Pastors," *Christianity Today*, April 30, 2018 https://www.christianitytoday.com/news/2018/april/paige-patterson-divorce-domestic-abuse-swbts-cbmw.html; Kate Shellnut, "Paige Patterson fired by Southwestern, stripped of retirement benefits," *Christianity Today*, May 30, 2018, https://www.christianitytoday.com/news/2018/may/paige-patterson-fired-southwestern-baptist-seminary-sbc.html.

42. See in particular, Sarah Pulliam Bailey, "Southern Baptist seminary drops bombshell: why Paige Patterson was fired," *Washington Post*, June 1, 2018, www.washingtonpost.com/news/acts-of-faith/wp/2018/06/01/southern-baptist-seminary-drops-bombshell-why-paige-patterson-was-fired/?utm_term=.395bb6984ae4.

43. Beth Moore, "A Letter to My Brothers," *The LPM Blog*, Living Proof Ministries, May 3, 2018, https://blog.lproof.org/2018/05/a-letter-to-my-brothers.html. All the following quotes are taken from this letter.

44. Melanie McAlister, "How Beth Moore is helping to change the face of evangelical leadership" *Washington Post*, June 22, 2018, https://www.washingtonpost.com/news/post-nation/wp/2018/06/22/beth-moore-is-challenging-and-helping-to-change-the-face-of-evangelical-leadership/?utm_term=.bdb1c153b155.

Dr. Kevin Giles, an Australian, has served as an Anglican parish minister for over forty years. He has been publishing on the substantial equality of the sexes since 1975. He holds a doctorate in New Testament studies and has published books on the church, church health, ministry in the apostolic age, the book of Acts, gender equality, and the Trinity, and numerous scholarly and popular articles.

JAMIN HÜBNER

The Nashville Statement: A Critical Review

It is not every day that a document about theology and gender makes national news. The "Nashville Statement," however, accomplished this very thing in September of 2017.¹ The document, issued by the Council for Biblical Manhood and Womanhood (CBMW), is identified as "A Coalition for Biblical Sexuality" and intends to set the record straight with regard to human identity, transgenderism, homosexuality, and other related topics.

The initial response to the Statement was extensive, both in and outside the Christian community. Discussion about the Statement has since died down, but the debates surrounding ethics and gender/sexuality certainly have not. In any case, there has been little interaction with the Statement beyond popular commentary. What follows is a more detailed analysis surrounding the document in hopes of shining a brighter light on this controversial topic. The plan is to frame the debate, systematically examine the Statement itself, and conclude with final reflections.

The Deep Context of the Nashville Statement

A number of contextual layers stand behind the Nashville Statement (henceforth NS). For example, the *socio-political* context reveals that the NS came just two years after the landmark Supreme Court decision favoring same-sex marriage. This event, viewed by many as emblematic of the decline of "Judeo-Christian values," has left many evangelicals on edge, thus prompting, in part, the production of the NS. "It would be much easier to be quiet," wrote Albert Mohler in The *Washington Post* on the NS, "to let the moral revolution proceed unanswered, and to seek some kind of refuge in silence or ambiguity . . . we did not believe we could remain silent." [2]

The *socio-theological* context is another important layer. The NS is essentially a sequel to the 1987 Danvers Statement on gender roles.[3] Both were written by the same organization and endorsed by many of the same professors, pastors, and authors. The Danvers Statement provided the necessary framework for the NS, including specific content, such as Art. 1, 3, and 4 (which address the differences between man and woman). What, then, is CBMW?

CBMW was established to counteract the progress of secular feminism and Christian feminism and egalitarianism.[4] CBMW refers to its own views on the subject as "complementarianism," which asserts permanent, differentiating gender roles for each sex. The term itself has been shown to be misleading because the meaning of "role" has been misconstrued[5] and because complementarianism amounts not to complementarity as much as hierarchy. Female subordination to male authority is considered the divine arrangement between the sexes.[6] As a result, women are restricted from leadership positions in various spheres of society, though the extent of which remains debated by CBMW proponents.[7] Additionally, discourse about God (which is primarily metaphorical/figurative) should be restricted to masculine language—even though the Christian Scriptures do not exhibit such monolithic descriptions.[8]

This primacy of maleness is perhaps evident in the NS and its list of original signers. The document was written by men and endorsed mostly by men. Out of the handful of female signers, several include their "complementarian roles" (e.g., "homemaker," "president's wife") above professional employment positions, whereas there is no equivalent for male signers (e.g., "breadwinner," "husband of x"). And, as explained below, depictions of God and other topics are needlessly (and unhelpfully) gendered—and in masculine terms.

As a "Council," CBMW's members and participants see themselves not merely as providing an alternative to prevailing opinions, but as establishing the absolute, unquestionable, objective, timeless, biblical truth about manhood and womanhood. Just as the Councils of Nicaea (325) and Constantinople (381) summarized the gospel story and defined basic Christology, so the CBMW has decreed what it means to be a man and a woman (1987) and, now, how that theological anthropology works out more specifically (2017). As Mohler comments, "The 'Nashville Statement,' *like many other doctrinal declarations common to Christian history*, seeks to summarize, clarify, and affirm what Holy Scripture reveals."[9]

A third layer is the *historical-theological context*. In brief, the NS is a product of religious fundamentalism.[10] "Found in versions of Islam, Hinduism, and Buddhism as well as Christianity, religious fundamentalism typically (though not always or exclusively) displays such characteristics as an unusually expansive concept of "orthodoxy,"[11] simplistic or undeveloped binary thinking,[12] a separatist ethos,[13] a warfare or fortress mentality,[14] apocalypticism or alarmism/extreme urgency,[15] stigma towards broad learning,[16] groupthink,[17] pseudo-scholarship,[18] cult-personalities or extreme admiration of assertive authority figures,[19] proselytism/triumphalism,[20] self-legitimization,[21] an obsession with certainty,[22] textual idolatry (e.g., biblicism and bibliolatry[23]),[24] and foundationalist epistemology.[25]

The initial endorsements to the NS—supplemented by short comments of other proponents—demonstrate most of these features:[26]

- **Biblicist Foundationalist Epistemology**: "[The NS] is *built* on the persuasion that the Christian Scriptures speak with clarity and authority for the good of humankind" (John Piper); "The Nashville Statement's doctrinal affirmations are technically correct, in the way that a house built on sand might be architecturally correct" (*First Things*)[27]; "my prayer is that it will help anchor churches and Christians" (Russell Moore).
- **Apocalypticism/Urgency/Alarmism**: "In the present generation, confusion and perversion surrounding gender, marriage, and human sexuality continue

to define our times" (Jason Allen); "It touches the most fundamental and urgent questions of the hour" (Piper); The NS "is an urgently needed moment of gospel clarity" (Moore); "In our day truth is being forsaken in this arena . . ." (Ligon Duncan); "This is one of those moments in which the church must stand and not fall . . . these are some of the most controversial issues of our time" (Mohler); "Gender confusion is rampant and lives are being damaged as a result" (Akin); "The velocity of cultural change in recent years has left many Christians perplexed" (Jeff Purswell); "believers must take a stand for the Word of God. . . . in a time of cultural confusion over complex matters" (Thomas White); "We believe that human dignity, human flourishing, and true human freedom are at stake" (Mohler).[28]

- **Warfare/Fortress Mentality**: "To capitulate to the spirit of the age . . . would be to abandon the mission field. . . . The church must stand ready" (Moore); "a torrid assault in the cultural climate of our day" (Daniel Akin); "We must stand our ground on the unchanging Word of God. . . . The Nashville Statement is courageous" (Burk Parsons); "calling us to stand faithfully for him" (Ray Ortlund); "The Nashville Statement . . . will equip believers to respond to such issues with courage. . . ."

- **Simplistic Binarism**: "In order to be truly for the world, when the world is going the wrong way, you must be against the world" (Jerry Johnson); "people who have a problem with the Nashville Statement have a problem with God and His Word. It's that simple" (Michael Brown);[29] "[NS] has incited those who would replace Christianity with a new religion teaching a new morality to be explicit in their rejection of the historic Christian faith"[30] (Mohler); "two rival visions of what it means to be human are now fully apparent" (Mohler).

- **Expanded Orthodoxy**: "I am signing The Nashville Statement because I stand with Biblical orthodoxy" (Rosaria Butterfield); "on the most basic truth of what it means to be human" (Mohler); "It declares the very heart of Christianity" (Ortlund); "confusion reigns over some of the most basic questions of our humanity" (Denny Burk); "just the most basic of the basics" (Brown).[31]

- **Proselytism/Triumphalism**: "we have articulated what God's Word says about issues of sexuality and gender" (Akin); "The Nashville Statement clearly articulates evangelical beliefs on biblical sexuality" (White); "Like so many other statements . . . we'll look back on The Nashville Statement as a word that needed to be said, a message that needed to be sent. It is clarity in the midst of confusion that will stand the test of time and the test of truth" (Mohler).
- **Self-legitimization**: "the vitriol in response to our document showed why such clarification is necessary. . . . The backlash to the document shows why it is so needed. . . . The very fact that the statement made headlines and was greeted with shock and surprise in some quarters underlines why it was needed" (Mohler);[32] "It is courageous" (Kevin DeYoung).
- **Biblicism**: "these other 'Christian' leaders have rejected the authority of the Word of God. . . . the statement only reaffirms what the Bible clearly teaches" (Brown); "summary of basic biblical categories, rooted in sound exegesis, and an over-all commitment to the consistency of Scripture as a divine revelation" (James White).[33]

All of this shows that the NS emerges out of a particular ideology and cultural ethos. It is not religiously, ideologically, or culturally neutral. It is not "mere Christianity."

A fourth contextual lens—the most important in our case—is the context of *systematic theology*. American fundamentalism was forged out of a myriad of conflicts in the early 1900s surrounding evolution, higher biblical criticism, fracturing denominations, modern optimism about human reasoning, and a myriad of other developments. This "fundamentalist-modernist controversy" has deeper roots in earlier Enlightenment expressions of Christian thought such as English Puritanism and post-Reformation scholasticism.

These roots have a direct bearing on the contents and presentation of the NS. Some of the vocabulary is nearly copied-and-pasted from such documents as *The Westminster Confession of Faith* (1646) or from contemporary proponents of such theologies (e.g., Piper, a CBMW leader and initial NS signer). The first paragraph of the NS, for instance, says "God created human beings for his glory," and then later in the Preamble, "God's design and his way of salvation serve to bring him the greatest glory and bring us the greatest good." This is essentially a restatement from *The Westminster Confession* (II.2-3, IV.1, V.1) and, more plainly, from the first part of the *Westminster Shorter Catechism*: "Man's chief end is to glorify God, and to enjoy him forever." Whether these ideas and terminology are properly implemented in the context of CBMW's views is debatable.

Less explicit implementation of Protestant thought includes phrases such as "God's holy purposes in creation and redemption," mentioned twice in Art. 7. The words "in creation" and "redemption," of course, are not referring to verses from the Bible but pointing to conceptual categories in systematic theology. The same is true for "the Fall" in Art. 4 (oddly capitalized, since other terms such as covenant, church, creation, and redemption are lowercase).

These are but samples of specific vocabularies, theological categories, and models of theology from the past five hundred years that make an appearance in the NS. As one would expect, there is a *particular theology* to a theological document. But, contrary to the assumptions of the authors of the NS, not all Christians agree with these theological constructs or with what their implementation would entail. Even the simple "creation-fall-redemption" schema (present, but not explicit, in the NS) has been critiqued in the past quarter century by a variety of theologians because it excises almost all of the OT and some of the NT. "Fall" is also fading out of use in order to better conform with a more biblical orientation (e.g., "alienation").[34]

There is much in the NS about Adam and Eve, creation, fall, redemption, and marriage as "covenant," but little about Israel and Israel's covenant, the New Covenant in the Messiah, peace, reconciliation, respect, or even love (except for a passing remark about speech in Art. 11, and a specific analogy for marriage in Article 1).[35] There is also little about pertinent topics like abuse and violence and their opposition to the gospel. Again, the theological orientation is *peculiar*. This is not simply due to the subject matter—as if homosexuality and transgenderism somehow require more talk about God's glory, obedience, and Eph 5 than about God's patience, faithfulness, or 1 Cor 7.

The NS did not emerge out of a timeless, theological vacuum. While it is supposed to be an objective, universally-binding, eternal re-presentation of unchanging divine truths, the NS remains best described as an American evangelical fundamentalist quasi-reformed perspective on gender written primarily by white American male Protestants. It would be unwise to use it as a litmus test for global orthodoxy.

A fifth and final layer is the *literary* context of the NS. Just as "one does not simply walk into Mordor," so one does not simply write a statement of faith. Documents like the NS are a specific literary phenomenon that can be traced back to ancient creeds and confessions. The purposes of each creed, confession, or formal "statement of faith" or "declaration" vary, but still entail a number of common features.[36] There is an *art and craft* to creed-writing and constructing formal declarations, and *genre* determines the boundaries and rules of interpretation. These boundaries serve as the basis for communicative success, limiters of meaning, purpose, standards of accuracy, etc.

Authorial intent is also important, though few creeds, confessions, and statements are written by a single author. They tend to be *composite* documents. Some material is a synthetic or hybrid construction that cannot be easily traced to any single author at all. The origins of the NS's various parts are likely never to be completely revealed, nor do they necessarily need to be. For if such source and redaction criticism *were* required to discern its content, this would nullify the belief of the authors themselves—that the NS is functionally prepared for mass consumption.

Nevertheless, literary origins can complicate specifics. Why, for instance, is "human identity" used in the Preamble and not "self-conception," but in the Articles "self-conception" *is* used but not "human identity"? Was this reversal of vocabulary intentional, a failure of the final editor to ensure consistency, or are "human identity" and "self-conception" radically different concepts in the authors' minds? And why is "people who experience sexual attraction for the same sex" used only to identify homosexuals in Art. 8 but not elsewhere where homosexuals are referenced? (To make room for bisexuals, perhaps?) And, why is there only one biblical quotation or citation in the entire document (Matt 19:12 in Art. 6)? Such questions point to some of the disadvantages of disembodied, corporately-authored public statements.

There are also different subsets under this broad genre. The NS tends toward "a standard, a battle cry, a testimony and witness to the world,"[37] as opposed to a tool for liturgy, a guide for memorizing doctrine, or a basis for catechism. One should therefore not fault the NS for being difficult to memorize, ineloquent, or failing as an effective pedagogical tool. Even here there are looming concerns because the signers do not all agree on why exactly the NS was written. Piper says, "The aim . . . is to shine a light into the darkness—to declare the goodness of God's design in our sexuality and in creating us as male and female."[38] Mohler spreads the tent far wider: "The main goal . . . is to point all persons, regardless of the form of our struggles over sexuality or self-identity, to salvation and wholeness in Christ."[39] That is, the document is actually a call toward salvation. Russell Moore's delineation, on the other hand, is much more complex.[40]

These differences—even if minor—further complicate the task of interpretation. Because both author and reader want a clear statement of purpose, this pushes readers in the direction of *caution* when reading it—and even more caution when *applying* it. But this might nullify the entire project since it is meant to establish an official benchmark that requires minimal guesswork. The authors therefore appear overly-optimistic about what a single public statement can accomplish.

Just as important is the distinction between what is said and *how* it is said—between the content of something and its form (e.g., rhetoric, literary structure, tone, rhythm, etc.).[41] This is particularly noteworthy since the *effect* of the NS has invoked the harshest criticism. For a document addressing gender in the twenty-first century, this aspect is particularly important. It goes without saying that the proponents of the NS believe that success has already been achieved on this mark. Before the NS was exposed to the global church, it was judged to have "compassion" and to be "gracious" (Piper), "compassionate," "pastorally wise" (Grudem), a "loving statement" (DeYoung), a "compassionate affirmation" (Parsons), expressed "lovingly" (Duncan) and with "compassion" (Akin, White), and even "breathtakingly glorious" (Ortlund).[42] However, we should note that these are not the kind of judgments the signers can accurately make before public release; they are judgments for *others* to make *after* its release.

This problem of perception is another challenge of such public-statements. It is impossible to ensure that the effect of any written document will be the same for all audiences, "When we make declarations like this," writes one Southern Baptist, "we speak in the global language of sound bites, which leads to misunderstanding."[43] This is one of the biggest risks of attempting to speak for all people, once and for all—as opposed to, say, local pastors speaking in their own words for their own congregations, or simply writing a more modest declaration. As one professor and popular commentator notes,

> To utter these public pronouncements without an enveloping pastoral context fails to provide pastors with a loving context to these views. [44]

In short, there is no "one size fits all" creed, confession, or statement that is immune from criticism or from the changes of time and language. This is why multiple translations and versions of the Nicene Creed (and others) exist. And if *the Bible itself* can be regularly updated in different translations to fix dead metaphors, odd renderings, implement new scholarship, and reflect changes in language and culture, this basic aspect of changeability should not be too much to ask for something like the NS.

It should be noted that this situatedness of (all) literature is inevitable and does not preclude the possibility of communicating localized truths, accurate propositions, or cross-cultural facts.[45] But it is disturbing that there are no phrases like "this is but an attempt," or "all statements like this are provisional," or "our context limits our perspective," or "this might have varying nuance in another culture." There are not even caveats like "we are open to correction," or "we hope to talk about this with others," or "we surely have blind spots." Perhaps, then, if there is any sin of omission in the NS, it is not so much a missing Article or two, but a humble recognition of basic human creatureliness.[46] The authors do not squarely acknowledge the inherent limitations of sinful people drawing an immovable line in the sand, nor do they find it necessary to make such an acknowledgement.

Preamble

The Preamble to the NS is remarkably similar to the 2006 preface of the book, *Recovering Biblical Manhood and Womanhood*.[47] The focus is on a cultural worldview shift, and reform is stressed. There are also a number of pressing concerns.

For example, we read, "It is common to think that human identity as male and female is not part of God's beautiful plan, but is, rather, an expression of an individual's autonomous preferences." This statement is likely a false dichotomy. As will be explored below, identifying as male or female *is frequently part* of God's plan and design, not necessarily opposed to it. In fact, in the biblical narrative (given certain conditions) what God plans and what people choose are often one and the same.[48] Additionally, the sheer number of ways in which femininity and masculinity can be expressed—both in and outside the human species—suggests that God loves variety in precisely this corner of creation. Whether there are *limitations* to such variety (either by ability or by ethical norms) is another debate. But to simply pit God's plan against human free choice is framing the whole document as "humans vs. God," which will likely limit the NS's capacity to speak effectively.

A sort of pseudo-theological patriarchy embedded in the Preamble begins to emerge—"*his* glory," "*his* creatures," "to *him* alone," "made us for *himself*," etc. The church is "her," "she," and is meant to "bring him the greatest glory." That this choice of gendered language (and metaphors) is stressed so persistently in such a short preface is peculiar—especially given the plain (and needlessly) patriarchal picture it portrays. Might there be a more helpful and sensitive depiction of God? Some readers of this preface might find gentle Jesus, "friend of sinners," the oppressed slave who carries our burdens, much easier to relate to than the more distant "Creator and Lord of all" to whom "every person owes gladhearted thanksgiving, heart-felt praise, and total allegiance."[49] This collection of metaphors and models (masculine, militaristic, unidirectional) is not illegitimate as much as *misplaced*—especially if the authors want to persuade their audience instead of pressuring them to surrender and worship. One recalls the words of two Reformed theologians: Daniel Migliore, who says, "God's grace is not coercive but gives humanity time,"[50] and Herman Bavinck, "covenant honors the fact that God created men and women as rational and moral beings. He treats us as such by not coercing us but using persuasion; he wants us freely and willingly to serve him in love (Ps. 100:3f.)."[51] Perhaps the overall tone and choice of words might be different with these theological reflections in mind.

For better or worse, a fuller black-and-white model takes shape in the Preamble: "Will the church of the Lord Jesus Christ lose her biblical conviction, clarity, and courage, and blend into the spirit of the age? Or will she hold fast to the word of life, draw courage from Jesus, and unashamedly proclaim his way as the way of life?" Christians who have not lost conviction and courage, but also have trouble living and proclaiming God's way of life, are excluded from these either/or options. And what about those who simply need space to think about the complex topics of gender and homosexuality? Where might they fit in this dualism?

"We are persuaded that faithfulness in our generation means declaring once again the true story of the world and of our place in it—particularly as male and female." What is meant by "true story of the world" and "once again"? The church is, indeed, unanimous throughout history about the restriction of sexual activity to the bonds of heterosexual marriage.[52] Yes, there are good biblical and theological reasons for continuing to uphold this perspective. But, this is not what the NS is truly about, as it also includes big theories of theological anthropology and psychology, gender (and transgender), biology, theology, ethics—and a specific relation among all of these. On *this* wide variety of topics, there is no single "true story" prior to the present age. For example, the topic of marriage itself was a loose-steering wheel throughout church history, some praising singleness and celibacy, others marriage and children.[53] The same goes for sexual activity—in some Christian expressions, never in excess and only for procreation, while in other expressions it was viewed quite the opposite.[54] There is even more lack of consensus about biology and gender, psychology, and anthropology.

Indeed, the majority of the views in the NS cannot be called "traditional" any more than all the views about gender in The Danvers Statement are "traditional."[55] This is partly because matters such as transgenderism, "self-conception" and/or "human identity," and the relationship between biological sex and gender have not been topics of discussion for most of church history.[56] How, then, can the NS be relaying a tradition that did not exist? The claim to "tradition" also does not hold because of the high level of nuance associated with these topics, which cannot be identified with more than a handful of contemporary, like-minded authors (many, ironically, who are signers of the NS). Some perspectives (or at least specific articulations) in the NS may, in fact, approach innovation.[57] In a word, then, *the NS is the result of doctrinal development and recent human innovation, not merely the repetition of some earlier Christian tradition.*

Immediately following the theologically-selective call to allegiance,[58] the Preamble says, "This is the path not only of glorifying God, but of knowing ourselves." The definite article ("*the* path") is notable, because there seems to be little reason why the authors could not have said (to use one example), "God alone is Savior, Lover, and Friend of all who accept Jesus of Nazareth through personal trust; in this faithful Protector and Helper, we can become whole." It is unclear why a different yet theologically-sound alternative like this would be unacceptable.

Other remarks in the Preamble approach incredulity. "God's good plan provides us with the greatest freedom." According to CBMW, we recall that this "freedom" means that half the global church is prohibited from teaching men on Sunday mornings, preaching sermons to their own congregations, or engaging in any number of (arbitrary) activities solely on the basis of sex.[59] One therefore reads statements like these with as much seriousness as, for example, the Saudi Arabian government talking about the freedom of their female citizens (who were not even allowed to drive until 2017).

Readers are also reassured, "He [God] is for us and not against us." One wonders who "us" refers to and why this reassurance is necessary if the tone and content of the NS are adequate to demonstrate this. Whatever the case, the fundamentalist subtext here is plain, though this does not make it less disturbing when made explicit: "If you're for God, you're for the NS; if you're against the NS, you're against God."

Article 1

> *WE AFFIRM that God has designed marriage to be a covenantal, sexual, procreative, lifelong union of one man and one woman, as husband and wife, and is meant to signify the covenant love between Christ and his bride the church.*
>
> *WE DENY that God has designed marriage to be a homosexual, polygamous, or polyamorous relationship. We also deny that marriage is a mere human contract rather than a covenant made before God.*

Following in the footsteps of the Danvers Statement (which followed in the footsteps of the Chicago Statement on Biblical Inerrancy), the Articles are in an Affirmation-Denial format. Sometimes this approach adds clarity, while at other times it adds confusion.

This first Article contains several observations that any Christian might readily affirm. But three problems (and potential others) come to the surface: (a) defining marriage strictly as sexual and procreative (because many marriages may *not* be sexual, procreative, or either); (b) defining the essence of marriage according to a single analogy used rarely in the NT (which, ironically, could be misconstrued as promoting homosexuality, if pushed too far, since male Christians—as the "bride"—are marrying Christ); (c) the dualism of "mere contract" vs. "covenant made before God," perhaps implying that a marriage between non-Christians is invalid. Depending on one's perspective, the lack of qualifications here may appear careless.

Article 2

> *WE AFFIRM that God's revealed will for all people is chastity outside of marriage and fidelity within marriage.*
>
> *WE DENY that any affections, desires, or commitments ever justify sexual intercourse before or outside marriage; nor do they justify any form of sexual immorality.*

This Article is one of the least controversial and least complicated. Its perspective does not appear substantially problematic, including implications for homosexuality; a theological or biblical case for ethical homoeroticism is very difficult case to make.[60] Potential issues might arise over the use of "ever" (definitiveness proclaimed by human beings is often doubtful) and the boundaries of "sexual immorality."

Article 3

> *WE AFFIRM that God created Adam and Eve, the first human beings, in his own image, equal before God as persons, and distinct as male and female.*

WE DENY that the divinely ordained differences between male and female render them unequal in dignity or worth.

Sexual differentiation is, indeed, a blessing—as so much of creation's variety is. One might also affirm the thrust of the Denial, were it not written from a female-subordinationist perspective. The differences between male and female are not defined in the NS, but in the Danvers Statement. Any criticism directed at the Danvers Statement on this particular issue would apply here. In fact, if one expanded the Denial, the irony of complementarian anthropology becomes apparent: "we deny that [permanent subordination of women] renders them unequal in dignity or worth."[61]

Article 4

WE AFFIRM that divinely ordained differences between male and female reflect God's original creation design and are meant for human good and human flourishing.

WE DENY that such differences are a result of the Fall or are a tragedy to be overcome.

The same concerns highlighted for Art. 3 can be raised here. Restated according to its internal hierarchical perspective, we read that "permanent female subordinationism of women to men . . . is meant for human good." Readers of the NS—especially women—might legitimately be personally offended by such grotesqueries. Thoughtful readers may also find these tropes incredible, since they are claimed to be on par with divine truth, as well as "compassionate" and "careful" theological discourse.

Article 5

WE AFFIRM that the differences between male and female reproductive structures are integral to God's design for self-conception as male or female.

WE DENY that physical anomalies or psychological conditions nullify the God-appointed link between biological sex and self-conception as male or female.

This Article requires lengthy commentary beyond the scope of this review, so my remarks will be brief.

The thrust of the Affirmation seems to be that male/female organs should align with one's identity as male or female, but that this identity ("self-conception") must also be according to "God's design." The thrust of the Denial seems to be that intersexuality, bisexuality, or transgender phenomena[62] does not trivialize the alignment between biological maleness/femaleness and gender (identifying as "male/female")—which, again, is "God-appointed/designed." In other words, those who are biologically male should always identify as men and behave like men according to complementarian standards, and those biologically female should always identify and behave as women according to complementarian standards.

The first problem is that "biologically" can have at least two meanings: genetic and reproductive. Genetic (chromosomal) sex is "permanent" after conception. But reproductive sex is not so fixed—as witnessed by the rare (but real) cases of intersexuality. The Affirmation explicitly refers to "reproductive structures," so it would seem that the reference to "biological sex" in the Denial means the same. Thus the very existence of intersexuality renders the Denial—or at least its *intended purpose*—superfluous. That is, intersexual persons, given their dual reproductive structures (assuming this particular sense of intersexuality for the moment), have an obligation to behave in *both* masculine and feminine "roles." But this approach is impossible (or at least heretical) in CBMW's complementarian framework, which has no room for such people. Intersexual persons therefore are not capable of fulfilling "God's design," at least not without potentially dangerous surgery (among other changes). This raises questions about the meaning of "creation" and being "created" in general, since it no longer refers to the actual creation of individuals in the womb, but to a loaded theological construct.

Also, one might say that bisexual persons do not break the "link" between sex and gender but *add* a link to it (i.e., "two links," though not parallel except in cases of intersexuality).[63] How, then, is this statement meaningful for non-intersexual bisexuals?

It is here that we realize why public formal pronouncements on complex ethical topics *with theology* are so risky: the marginalized who are supposed to find help are instead rendered incapable of pleasing their own Maker. In the end, the attitude is not so much "come just as you are" as "come just as you are . . . post-op" or "come just as you are . . . if you can pretend to be more attracted to the opposite sex than your own."

Article 6

> WE AFFIRM that those born with a physical disorder of sex development are created in the image of God and have dignity and worth equal to all other image-bearers. They are acknowledged by our Lord Jesus in his words about "eunuchs who were born that way from their mother's womb." With all others they are welcome as faithful followers of Jesus Christ and should embrace their biological sex insofar as it may be known.
>
> WE DENY that ambiguities related to a person's biological sex render one incapable of living a fruitful life in joyful obedience to Christ.

The issue of implied readership and rhetorical effect is key in this Article. Imagine someone saying, "we affirm those born with only one leg are created in the image of God." What is the desired response to this line of thought? As Preston Sprinkle puts it, "'WE AFFIRM that Asian-Americans fully possess the image of God and can live joyful lives Him.' Well sure, but do we need to say this as if it's questionable?"[64]

The authors seem unaware of how these statements could be (and are) perceived. Such attempts to be affirming are actually patronizing. From what moral position do the authors feel inclined to allow the dignity of other persons and to assume others' gratitude because of it? [65] In this regard, the NS might actually be self-defeating. It is hoping to be a relevant engagement with the issues of the day, but instead fulfills precisely those contemporary fears of its own audience. Mohler's disclaimer, "We have no right to face the world from a claim of moral superiority," [66] ameliorates little because this appears to be precisely the presupposition behind the NS and the attitude within it.[67]

Perhaps the most insightful commentary on this Article is the reading of Christian intersexual persons themselves. Consider the story of "Lianne":

> "*and should embrace their biological sex insofar as it may be known*" means that intersex people should embrace the sex assigned them by doctors and accept

the medical treatment involved. This is the way I, as a Christian intersex person, understand their position. As do my intersex friends. We are castrated by doctors, undergo cosmetic sex assignment surgeries without our consent, are given hormones, lied to, have secrets kept from us, and made to live in shame. . . . That's what their statement means to us.[68]

Furthermore, what if the physicians were *mistaken* in their initial assignment (as it was for one of my wife's counseling clients)?[69] Does the NS require such a person to file for divorce, empty the bank account for surgery, and try to start a new life under a new name? Can this indeed be construed as "the path" to "human flourishing"?

The "clarity" of the NS seems to escape precisely those complex situations it was supposed to help. Warren Throckmorton, a Christian professor of psychology, accurately assesses the situation this way: "The real world of sexuality is not as neat and clean as portrayed by the signers of the Nashville Statement. I hope Lianne's story provides a caution to those who marginalize those who have been dealt a hand they didn't ask for."[70]

Article 7

WE AFFIRM that self-conception as male or female should be defined by God's holy purposes in creation and redemption as revealed in Scripture.

WE DENY that adopting a homosexual or transgender self-conception is consistent with God's holy purposes in creation and redemption.

The first line appears to be a (third) re-assertion of CBMW's complementarianism. But why should human identity (all the more, *Christian* identity) be defined solely in the categories of "creation and redemption" and not, for example, by the teachings of Jesus, or something else? Surely we cannot pass over the parables of Jesus or the Sermon on the Mount—with its Beatitudes, Lord's Prayer, and Golden Rule. The same might be asked about Paul's "fruit of the Spirit," one of the earliest Christian summaries of Christlikeness.

The Denial is confusing as well, since it implies that *simply identifying* as "homosexual" or "transgender," whether verbally or even in one's own mind, is unacceptable.⁷¹ (This assertion was made explicit in Art. 10 of the 2018 "Statement on Social Justice and the Gospel" by John MacArthur et al.: "We reject 'gay Christian' as a legitimate biblical category." ⁷²) The authors might as well have said, "WE DENY that recognizing oneself to be a sinner is consistent with God's holy purposes." But recall that Abram and Sarai were not called to immediately abandon polygamy before God would make a covenant with them, nor did God abandon covenant promises when the people of Israel clung to a hopeless system of monarchy and bloody political maneuvering (1 Sam 8).⁷³ The apostle Paul also had a self-conception of being "the greatest of sinners" (1 Tim 1:15; cf. Rom 7:15-25). In this sense, it is no more sinful to call oneself gay, straight, or lesbian than to call oneself greedy, arrogant, or violent.

Of course, "homosexuality" (set aside transgenderism for a moment) does not always refer to homoeroticism, anyway. "Homosexual" often refers to "those with same sex-attraction" (a psychological state) regardless of that person's social actions and/or sexual behaviors (an embodied social and ethical state). In that case, saying "I'm gay" is like saying "I find contemporary folk music to be beautiful" (though same-sex orientation is obviously more permanent and central). This is viewed as morally objectionable by the NS authors. But this is absurd. Are present-day disabled Christians to be charged with immorality for saying "I have MS?" or "I'm autistic?" Should they undergo "conversion therapy" and remain alienated from the local church in the meantime? I suggest that a genuinely Christian response to these questions is "no."

In short, the whole paragraph runs the risk of pushing some Christians into denial or back "in the closet." It does not see the church as a "hospital for sinners," or provide sound direction for the complexities of local congregations.⁷⁴

Article 8

> *WE AFFIRM that people who experience sexual attraction for the same sex may live a rich and fruitful life pleasing to God through faith in Jesus Christ, as they, like all Christians, walk in purity of life.*
>
> *WE DENY that sexual attraction for the same sex is part of the natural goodness of God's original creation, or that it puts a person outside the hope of the gospel.*

This Article has some of the same issues as Art. 7. The "us-them" mentality is more pronounced here. Regarding the last phrase of the Denial, one again wonders in what environment it would be required to say that those with same-sex attraction are not for this reason alone "going to hell" as it were.

The bigger issue is the internal tension: a person who experiences same-sex attraction can "live a rich and fruitful life pleasing to God" and "walk in purity" even though this experience is fundamentally contrary to "the natural goodness of God's original creation." Whether this is genuinely contradictory, one wonders why same-sex attraction is such a catastrophic problem for the Christian—so much that one should not even use a self-identifying word for it, and that one cannot *not* have an opinion about the subject without disassociating from Christianity (see Art. 10 below).

Article 9

> *WE AFFIRM that sin distorts sexual desires by directing them away from the marriage covenant and toward sexual immorality—a distortion that includes both heterosexual and homosexual immorality.*
>
> *WE DENY that an enduring pattern of desire for sexual immorality justifies sexually immoral behavior.*

This Article appears to be a corollary of what has been said before, and needs little by way of review.

Article 10

> *WE AFFIRM that it is sinful to approve of homosexual immorality or transgenderism and that such approval constitutes an essential departure from Christian faithfulness and witness.*
>
> *WE DENY that the approval of homosexual immorality or transgenderism is a matter of moral indifference about which otherwise faithful Christians should agree to disagree.*

This is perhaps the most controversial Article, since it implies that those who digress from the NS are not truly Christian. Proponents of the NS have explicitly said as much.[75] If this is the case, it is not entirely surprising since the same triumphalist claims have been made, by the same general constituency, about the Chicago Statement on Biblical Inerrancy[76] and the Danvers Statement.[77] If my narrative is correct, the NS essentially functions as the latest and greatest in a growing pile of lengthy fundamentalist theologically-correct documents—a litmus test for orthodoxy and a knife to wield for heresy-hunts.

The Denial doubles down on this polarizing approach. The authors say that not only homosexuality and transgenderism, but also that the *approval* of such matters, are not matters of moral indifference. It is as if the authors are inspired by the canons of the Second Council of Constantinople (AD 553), where condemnation was based on what and whom Christians condemn (e.g., "If anyone does not anathematize Arius . . . Eunomius, Macedonius, Apollinaris, Nestorius, Eutyches and Origen, together with their impious, godless writings, and all the other heretics . . . let him be anathema." [78]). Here, one falls under threat of church discipline or even excommunication for lacking or choosing not to voice an opinion about homosexuality or transgenderism. Granted, the NS will not be used for burning Christians at the stake. However, it *cannot* be said that this power play and the NS in general will not be used to hire and fire pastors, professors, and others.[79]

Another concern is that there are many types of transgenderism. Some intersexual persons might be categorized this way, or it might refer to others who have undergone surgery (whether intersexual or not), or to something less dramatic like prolonged cross-dressing. Paul's instructions in 1 Cor 11 and elsewhere assert that visible differentiation between the sexes should be maintained, for such creational variety is to be embraced and not suppressed. To re-incarnate the spirit of this instruction would require significant theological work, creativity, and wisdom. Christians in first-century Corinth (and elsewhere) were struggling with such issues as prostitution and prostitute converts to Christianity, marriages in which only one spouse becomes a Christian, and female slaves.[80] Today, the challenges include the possibility of sex-changes, the posited variety of gender orientations, and what constitutes an appropriate expression of femininity or masculinity.

But in its anti-intellectual biblicism, the NS ignores the implications of these differences precisely because they would open the door to alternative solutions regarding male-female authority structures. Since there cannot be options other than those presented in the NS, there is no theological, creative, wise work to be done, in the academy or in local churches. The public is simply told, in effect, to obey the Bible, sign on to such creeds as the NS, and ask no further questions because the answers have been officially dispensed.

Again, as mentioned earlier, the NS does not present itself as limited, contextualized, in development, or willing to hear alternative points of view in *or* outside of the church. It is a direct extension of God's mind; to question the NS is to question God.

Article 11

> *WE AFFIRM our duty to speak the truth in love at all times, including when we speak to or about one another as male or female.*
>
> *WE DENY any obligation to speak in such ways that dishonor God's design of his image-bearers as male and female.*

It is questionable whether the NS itself has fulfilled this article's affirmation. In any case, the Denial is particularly baffling. In what situation has someone suggested that it is *necessary* to speak in a way that dishonors *anything*? The Denial seems hypothetical and disconnected without any clear context.

Article 12

> *WE AFFIRM that the grace of God in Christ gives both merciful pardon and transforming power, and that this pardon and power enable a follower of Jesus to put to death sinful desires and to walk in a manner worthy of the Lord.*
>
> *WE DENY that the grace of God in Christ is insufficient to forgive all sexual sins and to give power for holiness to every believer who feels drawn into sexual sin.*

This Article affirms that all Christians with same-sex attraction have the capacity to change. While this may be the case for some individuals, it tends to be the exception and not the rule. What, then, of those who cannot seem to "kick" their same-sex attraction?

Given the Article, there appear to be five possible conclusions:

a. They are not truly Christian ("a follower of Jesus").
b. They are capable of changing their orientation but choose not to.
c. They are *resisting* the power and grace of God.
d. God has not given them power to overcome.
e. God's power and grace are inadequate.

Given the Article, (d) and (e) are not real options. From here, the situation gets more sophisticated because the contingency not clearly addressed is *under what conditions* such "power" is given. The last phrase of the Denial alludes to this caveat: it is "to every believer who feels drawn into sexual sin." But this may not be the same group addressed in the Affirmation. If it *is* the same group (which seems likely), then option (a), (b), or (c) would follow.

But each of these is problematic. If (a) is the case, every Christian with same sex-attraction who cannot ultimately overcome it is not truly a Christian. This is the same as saying that homosexuals cannot become Christians. The absurdity of this suggestion—especially given Christianity's diverse range of converts[81]—merits no further comment. If (b) is the case, one wonders why many more homosexual Christians do not change, since changing their orientation is merely a choice. Indeed, the debate about just how much one's orientation is a choice continues to rage.[82] It also seems overly simplistic and perhaps unjustly incriminating to reduce the entire state of affairs to the power of choice. If (c) is the case, then the failure to change one's life in this way is resisting God's power (see Art. 5). But it is not this simple, and it also conflicts with the enablement concept in the Article. Even if it were so simple, this would presumably result in grounds for some kind of admonishment (e.g., "I told you, stop being attracted to other people of the same sex; you're resisting God's power"), which would drive an unnecessary wedge[83] into the person's relational and spiritual life with God.[84] Such a confrontation is counter-intuitive, insensitive, lacking in pastoral wisdom, and likely not to lead to change.

Perhaps there are other conclusions than these five. But, it would appear on first glance that, no matter which way one cuts it, Art. 12 is not very encouraging or hopeful for homosexual persons who wish they did not have the struggles that they do.

Article 13

> WE AFFIRM that the grace of God in Christ enables sinners to forsake transgender self-conceptions and by divine forbearance to accept the God-ordained link between one's biological sex and one's self-conception as male or female.

> WE DENY that the grace of God in Christ sanctions self-conceptions that are at odds with God's revealed will.

The content of this Article has already been addressed above. There are different senses of "transgender," "biological sex," and (something we did not have time to explore) "link."[85] Suffice it to say that there is more opportunity here for confusion and discouragement than for clarity, understanding, and encouragement.

Article 14

> WE AFFIRM that Christ Jesus has come into the world to save sinners and that through Christ's death and resurrection forgiveness of sins and eternal life are available to every person who repents of sin and trusts in Christ alone as Savior, Lord, and supreme treasure.

> WE DENY that the Lord's arm is too short to save or that any sinner is beyond his reach.

It is unfortunate for such a straightforward doxology to conclude a document like the NS. It is the rhetoric of hearty words and a tone of hope, all after an unusually convoluted series of propositions on theology and gender. More hopeful is that many in the church can see through such language and rhetoric into what actually amounts to contemporary abuse of theology and theological language.

Conclusion

In 2006, a thirty-one year old Navy specialist underwent sex re-assignment surgery to become a woman; Fox Fallon then enrolled in women's cage fighting. In 2014, (s)he brutalized a female opponent, leaving her with a concussion and a damaged orbital bone—attributable (in part) to a clear physiological advantage. More recently, a man-to-woman transgender charged with rape sexually assaulted four women after being sent to an all-female prison.[86]

Is this, to borrow language from the NS, what it looks like for human beings to rebel against God's ordained design for man and woman in the twenty-first century? Is this what Abraham Kuyper meant by "Modernism, which denies and abolishes every difference, [and] cannot rest until it has made woman man and man woman"?[87] Perhaps it is. But if CBMW's Nashville Statement is supposed to provide an effective, persuasive, and decisive Christian response to such rare spectacles, it has a long way to go.

This assessment is even more true for the common situations involving homosexuality, bisexuality, and patriarchalism. Despite a handful of agreeable propositions, the NS generally confuses, patronizes, and exhibits an attitude of unidirectional power and control. There is not even a mention of the well-known abuses and mistreatment of girls, women, and LGBTQ persons by professing Christians and their leaders.[88] Nor is there any concession that "complementarian" or "traditional" gender roles simply do not fulfill their promises (i.e., self-identified evangelicals are as abusive and adulterous as those in secular culture). Instead, there is a polarizing morass of seemingly contradictory assertions, perplexing terms, simplistic assertions and above all, a morally disturbing subtext.

Now more than ever, the church should remember that actions speak louder than words. People feel loved when they are loved, not when they are simply *told* that they are loved. Positive change happens by authentic relationships embodying the Spirit of Christ, not by official documents passed down from a theologically narrow subset of primarily white American evangelicals. When the church is being Christ's body, onlookers will say as they did centuries ago: "Look . . . how they love one another . . . and how they are ready to die for each other."[89]

Notes

1. The Statement was featured in *The Washington Post*, *USA Today*, and *The New York Times*.
2. Albert Mohler, "I signed the Nashville Statement. It's an expression of love for same-sex attracted people," *Washington Post* (Sept 3, 2017).
3. See https://cbmw.org/uncategorized/the-danvers-statement/.
4. See "Our History," *CBMW*, https://cbmw.org/about/history/.
5. See Kevin Giles, "The Nicene and Reformed Doctrine of the Trinity," *Priscilla Papers* 31, no. 3 (Summer 2017): 3-8; Rebecca Groothuis, "Complementarianism--What's in a Name?," *Mutuality* 6 (Jan 1999).
6. See John Piper and Wayne Grudem, eds., *Recovering Biblical Manhood and Womanhood* (Wheaton: Crossway, 1991, new preface in 2006), and Köstenberger, *God, Marriage, and Family*.
7. Compare, for example, various interpretations and applications of 1 Tim 2 by complementarians in Jamin Hübner, "Revisiting the Clarity of Scripture and 1 Timothy 2:12," *JETS* 59, no. 1 (2016): 99-117, rev. and republished in *Priscilla Papers* 30, no. 3 (2016): 18-25.
8. E.g., Isa 31:5; 42:14; 49:14-15; 66:12-13; 46:3-4; Deut 32:11-12, 18; Hos 11:1-4; 13:8; Pss 17:8; 22:9-10; 36:7; 57:1; 71:6; 91:1, 4; 131:2; Job 38:8, 29; Prov 8:22-25; 1 Pet 2:2-3, Acts 17:28; Num 11:12, possibly 15; Neh 9:21; Isa 66:9; Luke 13:18-21;15:8-10 Matt 23:37; John 3:5; 1:13; 4:7; 5:1, 4, 18; 1 Thess 2:7, etc. Classic studies on this subject include the works of Elizabeth Schüssler Fiorenza, Rosemary Radford Reuther, Elizabeth Johnson, Sallie McFague, Janet Soskice, Phyllis Trible, and Serene Jones.
9. Mohler, "I signed the Nashville Statement." Emphasis mine.
10. On religious fundamentalism in general, see Sathianathan Clarke, *Competing Fundamentalisms: Violent Extremism in Christianity, Islam, and Hinduism* (Louisville: WJK, 2017); Peter Heriot, *Religious Fundamentalism* (New York: Rutledge, 2008), and Charles Kimball, *When Religion Becomes Evil* (New York: HarperOne, 2008). On American evangelical fundamentalism, see George Marsden, *Fundamentalism and American Culture* (New York: OUP, 2006), Nancy Murphy, *Beyond Liberalism and Fundamentalism: How Modern and Postmodern Philosophy Set the Theological Agenda* (New York: Continuum, 1996), and James Barr, *Fundamentalism* (Louisville: WJK, 1978), *idem, Escaping Fundamentalism* (London: SCM, 1985).
11. The list of "essentials" or "core doctrines" grows ever larger to include a variety of nuanced opinions. See Art. 10 below.
12. This includes a consistent "black and white" attitude and misunderstanding toward ideas that cannot be slated into a dualism of opposing sides.
13. Believing communities lack social integration, and hermeticism is validated by attempts not to be "stained by the world." There is pride in exclusion (e.g., "our church

is smaller than all those more popular ones—and this proves we are right; narrow is the gate"), and fear of building relationships across social, ethnic, sexual, linguistic, and religious boundaries (e.g., homophobia, xenophobia, etc.).

14. States of affairs are regularly described by war-time metaphors and analogies (e.g., "battle," "conquer," "win," "war," "soldier," "fight"). All conflict or difference of opinion is reduced to a set of competing propositions, as "those who are not for us are against us." This also includes defensive postures (e.g., forbidding all inter-religious dialogue).

15. "Now" is always the most desperate hour for the recovery of society. Hesitance in action is a sign of either weakness, moral culpability, or compromise. (Cf. Art. 10 below.)

16. Bible colleges are preferred over liberal arts colleges and public universities. Some entire fields (e.g., sociology, philosophy, religion) are viewed as generally threatening, as are historical and literary criticism of the Bible.

17. The desire for unity and harmony leads to irrational thinking and/or coercive attitudes, and constant re-affirmation of the same slogans, metaphors, models, or descriptors is needed to "protect the flock from wolves." Independent thinking apart from group consent, participation, or official approval is viewed with anxious concern.

18. Fake or faulty credentials are typical, as well as general or emphasized suspicion about mainstream academia and excessive appeal to anecdotes in argumentation. There is also a fundamental incapacity to distinguish non-binary categories and different types of data and arguments, an over-reliance on secondary sources and opinion, and an uncritical awareness of linguistic, social, and cultural situatedness.

19. Fundamentalist organizations tend to center around hierarchical leadership and monopolized channels of information, often leading to abuses of power and a domineering spirit.

20. Calls to tribal allegiance are equivocated as calls to more and spiritual faithfulness. Fear tactics are often used to induce shame and/or conversion, and there is a general assumption that the truth has been mastered and the remaining task is to distribute and defend it (i.e., privileging the apologetic).

21. Polemics is central and not peripheral; being the object of external criticism is twisted into proof of being right (galvanization). This category would also include cases of playing the victim/oppressed.

22. A variety of opinions obtain the same level of conviction and epistemological weight regardless of differences in intellectual support. Certainty is a general indicator of truth while doubt is a general indicator of falsehood. The refusal to possess conviction or certainty in certain areas is evidence of ideological/theological compromise and those who ask forbidden questions are viewed as potentially malevolent dissenters. Note that this topic was recently tackled by Gregory Boyd, *Benefit of the Doubt* (Grand Rapids: Baker, 2013) and Peter Enns, *The Sin of Certainty* (New York: HarperOne, 2016).

23. Like "fundamentalism," the term "bibliolatry" is not simply a pejorative

adjective but a meaningful term in religious studies. See Robert Van Voorst, *Anthology of World Scriptures*, 9th ed. (Boston: Cengage, 2016), 10, 20.

24. What one believes is regularly equivocated with "what the Bible says." Sacred texts are viewed as a storehouse of inerrant propositions and facts, where all genres are collapsed into "teaching" (hence the phrase, "the Bible teaches"). Furthermore, societal woes—including sexual immorality and ethical dysfunction—are automatically attributed to a "low view of the Bible." The words and text of scriptures become more important than what they actually communicate. See Carlos Bovell, *Inerrancy and the Spiritual Formation of Younger Evangelicals* (Eugene: Wipf and Stock, 2007); *idem, Interdisciplinary Perspectives on the Authority of Scripture* (Eugene: Wipf and Stock, 2011); *idem, Rehabilitating Inerrancy in a Culture of Fear* (Eugene: Wipf and Stock, 2012); James Dunn, *The Living Word* (Minneapolis: Fortress, 2003); Christian Smith, *The Bible Made Impossible: Why Biblicism is Not a Truly Evangelical Reading of Scripture* (Grand Rapids: Brazos, 2012), and James Barr, *Beyond Fundamentalism* (Louisville: WJK, 1984).

25. In addition to a naïve realist perspective, propositional language is privileged and all truths are considered linear extensions of certain "foundational" truths.

26. Unless noted, these quotations come from the CBMW website.

27. Samuel James, "The Nashville Statement's Imperfect Clarity," *First Things* (Sept 5, 2017).

28. Mohler, "I Signed the Nashville Statement."

29. Michael Brown, "Why the Rejection of the Nashville Statement is a Rejection of the Bible," *TownHall.com* (Sept 2, 2017).

30. Mohler, "I Signed the Nashville Statement."

31. Brown, "Why Rejection."

32. Mohler, "I Signed the Nashville Statement."

33. James R. White, public comment (Sept 5, 2017) posted on Preston Sprinkle, "My Nashville Statement," *PrestonSprinkle.com* (Sept 3, 2017), https://www.prestonsprinkle.com/blogs/theologyintheraw/2017/9/3/my-nashville-statement.

34. Thus, some would propose a "mega-narrative" of "Creation-Sin-Israel-Cross-Church-Consummation" or similar. On this debate and topic of "biblical theology" and theological interpretation, see N. T. Wright, *Scripture and the Authority of God* (New York: HarperOne, 2013); Craig Bartholomew, *Introducing Biblical Hermeneutics* (Grand Rapids: Baker, 2015); John Goldingay, *Biblical Theology* (Downers Grove: InterVarsity, 2017); Michael Bird, *Evangelical Theology* (Grand Rapids: Zondervan, 2013); Daniel Treier, *Introducing the Theological Interpretation of Scripture* (Grand Rapids: Baker, 2008); Francis Watson, *Text, Church, and World* (Edinburgh: T & T Clark, 1994). See also the "Current Issues in Theology" series (CUP), the "Reframing New Testament Theology" series (Abingdon), and the insights of Richard Plantinga, Thomas Thompson, and Matthew Lundberg, *An Introduction to Christian Theology* (Cambridge: CUP, 2010) for observations that deeply alter the work of systematicians.

35. As noted by Marsden, *Reforming Fundamentalism*, 148, in the perspective of fundamentalism, "When Christian leaders start talking about love or the limits of our knowledge, heresy cannot be far behind."

36. See Jaroslav Pelikan, *Credo* (New Haven: Yale University Press, 2005); John Leith, *Creeds of the Churches*, 3rd ed. (Louisville: WJK, 1982); Carl Trueman, *The Creedal Imperative* (Wheaton: Crossway, 2012).

37. Leith, *Creeds*, 9.

38. John Piper, cited in Nashville Statement Endorsements," *CBMW* (August 29, 2017). https://cbmw.org/topics/news-and-announcements/nashville-statement-endorsements/.

39. Mohler, "The Nashville Statement."

40. Moore's delineation is more complex: "The Sexual Revolution cannot keep its promises, and the church must stand ready to receive with compassion the many who are in need of a better hope. The Nashville Statement is part of that mission, and my prayer is that it will help anchor churches and Christians to the gospel of Jesus Christ for years to come." Cited in Denny Burke, "Nashville Statement Endorsements," *CBMW* (August 29, 2017), https://cbmw.org/topics/news-and-announcements/nashville-statement-endorsements/.

41. Cf. "locution" vs. "illocution."

42. Burke, "Nashville Statement Endorsements."

43. Bill Edmunds, "Letter: Is 'Nashville Statement' necessary?," *The Courier* (Sept 11, 2017).

44. "Scot McKnight, "The Nashville Statement: A Pastoral Approach," *Jesus Creed* (Sept 4, 2017), http://www.patheos.com/blogs/jesuscreed/2017/09/04/nashville-statement-pastoral-approach/#qFlfUf1u11O5HSbg.99

45. NS signer John Frame is well aware of this epistemological issue: "theology is not 'purely objective truth'; as we saw earlier, there is no such thing as purely objective truth, or 'brute fact.' Our theologies are not even the best formulations of truth-for-people for all times and places; Scripture is that. Our theologies are merely attempts to help people, generally and in specific times and places, to use Scripture better." John Frame, *The Doctrine of the Knowledge of God* (Phillipsburg: Presbyterian and Reformed, 1987), 80.

46. William Placher, *The Domestication of Transcendence* (Louisville: WJK, 1996), 181: "A basic lesson: theologians get in trouble when they think they can clearly and distinctly understand the language they use about God." Cf. Gordon Kaufman, *In Face of Mystery* (Cambridge: Harvard University Press, 1993).

47. Wayne Grudem and John Piper, eds., *Recovering Biblical Manhood and Womanhood*, 2nd ed. (Wheaton: Crossway, 2006, orig. 1991).

48. Placher, *The Domestication of Transcendence*, 111. Cf. Dorothy Soelle, *Thinking About God* (Eugene: Wipf and Stock, 2006), 190: "Transcendence is radical immanence." Cf. John Barclay, "Introduction," *Divine and Human Agency in Paul and*

His Cultural Environment, ed. Simon Gathercole and John Barclay (New York: T & T Clark, 2008), 7, who provides examples in the NT of this in action—God's activity *increasing* with more and more human action.

49. See Kaufman, *In Face of Mystery*; Sallie McFague, *Models of God* (Minneapolis: Fortress, 1987), *idem, Metaphorical Theology*; Joerg Rieger, *Christ and Empire* (Minneapolis: Fortress, 2007).

50. Daniel Migliore, *Faith Seeking Understanding*, 3rd ed. (Grand Rapids: Eerdmans, 2014), 298.

51. Migliore, *Faith Seeking Understanding*, 332.

52. See Preston Sprinkle, ed., *Two Views on Homosexuality, the Bible, and the Church* (Grand Rapids: Zondervan, 2016).

53. See Stanley Grenz, *Sexual Ethics* (Louisville: WJK, 1997).

54. See Peter Gardella, *Innocent Ecstasy* (New York: OUP, 1985).

55. Complementarianism proper—the idea that men and women are ontologically equal but functionally (teleologically) unequal in (permanent) authority roles—is a theological innovation of the 1970s and not a long-held tradition of the church (which in past centuries generally asserted women's inferiority).

56. Mohler indicates as much when saying, "we find ourselves clarifying what no previous generation of Christians has been called upon to clarify." Mohler, "I Signed the Nashville Statement."

57. This would not be unusual, as American fundamentalism has always been doctrinally innovative. Cf. George Marsden, *Reforming Fundamentalism* (Grand Rapids: Eerdmans, 1987), 5; and Kevin Giles, *Jesus and the Father: Modern Evangelicals Reinvent the Doctrine of the Trinity* (Grand Rapids: Zondervan, 2006).

58. On the use of "allegiance" in soteriology, see Jamin Hübner, review of Matthew Bates, *Salvation by Allegiance Alone* (Grand Rapids: Baker, 2016) in *The Canadian-American Theological Review* 6, no. 1 (2017): 121-27.

59. For a full delineation of this modern Pharisaism, see Wayne Grudem, *Evangelical Feminism and Biblical Truth* (Wheaton: Crossway, 2012, orig. 2004 by Multnomah), 2.7.

60. On the general issue of homosexuality, the Bible, and Christianity, see Robert Gagnon, *The Bible and Homosexual Practice* (Nashville: Abingdon, 2002); Nate Collins, *All But Invisible: Exploring Identity Questions at the Intersection of Faith, Gender, and Sexuality* (Grand Rapids: Zondervan, 2017); Preston Sprinkle, *People to be Loved: Homosexuality is Not Just an Issue* (Grand Rapids: Zondervan, 2015).

61. For more on this topic, see Adam Omelianchuk, "The 'Difference' Between 'A and Not-A': An Analysis of Alleged 'Word Tricks' and Obfuscations," *Priscilla Papers* 20, no. 1 (Winter 2006); idem, "Ontologically-Grounded Subordination: A Reply to Steven B. Cowan," *Philosophia Christi* 13, no. 1 (2011); 169-80; Rebecca Groothuis, "Equal in Being, Unequal in Role," in *Discovering Biblical Equality*, ed. Rebecca

Groothuis and Ronald Pierce, 2nd ed. (Downers Grove: InterVarsity, 2005), ch. 18.

62. "Intersexuality: the condition (such as that occurring in congenital adrenal hyperplasia or androgen insensitivity syndrome) of either having both male and female gonadal tissue in one individual or of having the gonads of one sex and external genitalia that is of the other sex or is ambiguous" (*Merriam-Webster's Dictionary*). "Bisexual: 1b: of, relating to, or characterized by sexual or romantic attraction to members of both sexes; also: engaging in sexual activity with partners of more than one gender" (*Merriam-Webster's Dictionary*). These categories do not necessarily exist binarily (yes/no), but in degrees. (E.g., someone can be strongly or mildly bisexual or homosexual.)

63. The substance of this "link" is not clear in the NS and could have a variety of meanings. On a related issue, it seems obvious that the ways in which sex/biology affects gender are numerous—as are the ways in which other variables (e.g., upbringing, social construction, cultural trends, mass advertising, theological ethics) affect gender. If it is the goal of the NS to address how much sex *should* determine/affect gender, that is not clear since the sex/gender distinction is not clearly established. In fact, the Statement seems intent on collapsing it altogether.

64. Preston Sprinkle, "My Nashville Statement."

65. More poignantly, is the global LGBTQ community significantly benefited by a group of white American male evangelicals publicly telling them that they have dignity and worth?

66. Mohler, "I Signed the Nashville Statement."

67. The proof-text is noticeably awkward. It is the only such case in the NS and is unnecessary at that (as if without these words of Jesus it would be questionable whether eunuchs, intersexual persons, and others are human beings).

68. Cited in Warren Throckmorton, "A Real Life Reason to Reject the Nashville Statement," *Patheos* (Sept 5, 2017), http://www.patheos.com/blogs/warrenthrockmorton/2017/09/05/reason-reject-nashville-statement/.

69. By "mistaken" in this situation and similar ones, I mean (a) the physician mistook the infant for (say) a male instead of intersex and/or (b) mistook the infant for a genetic male when the infant was genetically female.

70. Throckmorton, "A Real Reason."

71. It also (oddly) excludes bisexuals from the topic. It is unclear whether this was intentional.

72. John MacArthur, et al., "The Statement on Social Justice and the Gospel" (Sept 4, 2018), https://statementonsocialjustice.com/#affirmations-and-denials.

73. See Moshe Halbertal and Stephen Holmes, The Beginning of Politics: Power in the Biblical Book of Samuel (Princeton: Princeton University Press, 2017), in conjunction with the various works and commentaries of John Goldingay on this topic.

74. E.g., how to deal with a married gay couple who converted to Christianity. It does not work and is not wise for the pastors of that church to simply say, "You're

Christians now, so get divorced, turn over your children to a heterosexual family, and stop being attracted to those of the same sex."

75. See Brown, "Why the Rejection of the Nashville Statement is a Rejection of the Bible."

76. See the original publications of the International Council on Biblical Inerrancy.

77. See the works of Wayne Grudem on this subject.

78. Leith, *Creeds*, 50.

79. According to Mohler, Southern Baptist Theological Seminary plans to add the NS to its required documents of consent. See Kate Shellnutt, "Has Christian Psychology Lost Its Place at Southern Seminary?," *Christianity Today* (Sept 18, 2017).

80. See Cynthia Long Westfall, *Paul and Gender* (Grand Rapids: Baker Academic, 2015).

81. This is particularly true within the first and second centuries—where Christianity saw growth among eunuchs, homosexuals, prostitutes, Roman soldiers, and other minorities and unexpected groups.

82. In my view, it is difficult to argue that one's choice of sexual attractiveness is much different from what one finds attractive and beautiful outside human sexuality (art, music, etc.), and that such attraction can be changed by will-power.

83. Note, also, that 1 Cor 6:9 refers to homoeroticism, not homosexual orientation/attraction.

84. This admonishment would not be surprising given the nouthetic (admonishment) counseling methodology of the NS authors.

85. My own opinion is that both gender (masculinity, femininity, and everything in between) and gender orientation (gay, straight, bisexual, etc.) are jointly determined by social, ideological, psychological, and biological (i.e., sexual and hormonal) factors.

86. Martin Evans, Kate McCann, and Olivia Rudgard, "Transgender Person Accused of Rape is Remanded into Female Prison and Sexually Assaults Inmates within Days," *The Telegraph* (Sept 6, 2018).

87. Abraham Kuyper, *Lectures on Calvinism* (Grand Rapids: Eerdmans, 1987), 11.

88. Mohler, in *The Washington Times*, tried to briefly compensate for this glaring omission in his op-ed: "We know and confess that Christians have often failed to speak the truth in love."

89. Tertullian, cited in Krieder, *Patient Ferment* (Grand Rapids: Baker Academic, 2016), 58.

Dr. Jamin Andreas Hübner (ThD University of South Africa) is an academic, musician, and entrepreneur from South Dakota.

About CBE International

Leading Together, Serving as Equals

CBE International (Christians for Biblical Equality) advances the gospel by equipping Christians to use their God-given talents in leadership and service regardless of gender, ethnicity, or class.

CBE, a 501c3 nonprofit, is supported by a community that believes the Bible, properly interpreted, calls women and men to lead and serve as equals, based on Scriptures such as Galatians 3:28. Learn more.

Global Community

> Through CBE, "I learned men and women are equal. God did not curse [women], he cursed the ground. He did not curse those he loved, his own image. We must read the Bible holistically to understand it."
>
> —Youth pastor in Uganda

With supporters, ministry partners, and local chapters from over 100 denominations and 65 countries, CBE engages Christians with conferences, adult and youth curricula, multi-media resources, award-winning publications, a blog, and more.

CBE collaborates with pastors, churches, schools, and NGOs around the world to eliminate gender-based violence and human trafficking, and improve girls' access to education by raising the status of women.

Helping the Church Prevent Abuse

> "I am currently on the journey of recovering from [clergy] abuse and have a God-given passion to help speak into and resolve the issue in our churches…I enjoy the connection with CBE and the resources you provide."
>
> —Seminary student

In the US and around the world, 1 in 3 women are victims of physical abuse by an intimate partner, and studies show abuse is as common in the church as in society. CBE is working with church leaders to prevent abuse and create communities where women and men flourish as equals.

Healing and Hope

> "Thank you, quite literally, for my faith. Without CBE, at this point my very dear husband would be grieving terribly over my loss of faith."
> —CBE supporter

For more than 30 years, CBE's articles, books, and conferences have provided healing and hope for Christian women and men around the world.

To learn more about CBE, visit **cbe.today/about**.

Connect with CBE

To access award-winning articles, subscribe to our blog, check out our collection of egalitarian books, learn about CBE conferences, and more, visit **cbe.today/connect**.

www.cbeinternational.org

 facebook.com/cbeint   youtube.com/cbeinternational

 twitter.com/cbeint   soundcloud.com/cbe-international

www.ingramcontent.com/pod-product-compliance
Lightning Source LLC
Chambersburg PA
CBHW060201050426
42446CB00013B/2933